D1798109

DAWN AND DUSK

O quick quick quick, quick hear the song-sparrow,
Swamp-sparrow, fox-sparrow, vesper-sparrow
At dawn and dusk.

T. S. ELIOT *Cape Ann*

Dannie Abse
Kingsley Amis
W.H. Auden
George Barker
Frances Bellerby
John Betjeman
Thomas Blackburn
Roy Campbell
Charles Causley
Leonard Clark
T.S. Eliot
Roy Fuller
K.W. Gransden
Robert Graves
Michael Hamburger
John Heath-Stubbs
Geoffrey Hill
Kenneth Hopkins
Ted Hughes
Elizabeth Jennings
James Kirkup
Philip Larkin
Peter Levi
C. Day Lewis
Christopher Logue
Louis MacNeice
Edwin Muir
Norman Nicholson
Ruth Pitter
John Press
Herbert Read
James Reeves
Alan Ross
A.L. Rowse
Jon Silkin
Edith Sitwell
Osbert Sitwell
Stevie Smith
Stephen Spender
L.A.G. Strong
Hal Summers
Dylan Thomas
R.S. Thomas
Anthony Thwaite
Henry Treece
John Wain
Vernon Watkins
Laurence Whistler
David Wright
Andrew Young

Dawn and Dusk

POEMS OF OUR TIME

chosen and introduced by

CHARLES CAUSLEY

with designs by Gerald Wilkinson

BROCKHAMPTON PRESS

Also compiled by Charles Causley
Rising Early: 20th century ballads and story poems

All rights reserved. No part of this publication may be
reproduced or transmitted in any form or by any means,
electronic or mechanical, including photocopy, recording,
or any information storage and retrieval system, without
permission in writing from the publisher.
ISBN 0 340 15686 4
First printed 1962 Second impression 1964
Third impression 1966 Fourth impression 1968
Second edition 1972
Copyright © 1962 Charles Causley
Published by Brockhampton Press Ltd, Salisbury Road, Leicester
Printed in Great Britain
by Richard Clay (The Chaucer Press), Ltd, Bungay, Suffolk
Designer: Gerald Wilkinson

CONTENTS

5

3 CARNIVAL OF ANIMALS

4 PEOPLE AND PLACES

INTRODUCTION

True poets write poems because they must: not because they wish to impress their friends, or like to arrange words in new and striking ways, or (least of all) because they hope to make money. When the Welsh poet Dylan Thomas was asked to introduce a book of his collected poems, he said that he'd consider himself a fool if they were written, 'with all their crudities, doubts, and confusions,' for anything but the love of Man and in praise of God.

A lot of poetry fits all ages and all times. But the words of our present-day poets may also help us better to understand ourselves, each other, and the particular sort of world we happen to live in. The poet works continuously at the conveyor-belt of his imagination. As soon as he gets peace of mind at having completed one set of verses, fresh shapes are apt to rise in his head once more. And, if he is true to his art, he picks up his pen and goes on struggling to make something fresh in words of what he sees.

If the poet needs one special gift in addition to his own talents I'd say, as with all creative artists, that it is courage. For if he is to get immediately out of life what most other people get at second-hand out of a completed painting or symphony, novel or poem, he needs courage.

Most of the poems in this anthology, I think, speak for themselves. We must remember that all poems hint at many other worlds, thoughts, feelings, imaginings. A poem about a bird, for example, may have the whole of life contained in it as well as the bird. At certain times, of course, the reader must bring more to a poem than at others. The 'meaning' is something personal; it speaks to each of us alone. If we wish to work it out, we have to do so according to our own degree of sensibility. In doing so, we may also find that a marvellous fact about a good poem is that it will stand up, quite unshaken, to almost any number of interpretations.

Vernon Watkins said of his poem *The Collier* (page 80), 'The collier is not, in my conception, dead at the end of the poem, but recovering (in hospital probably) after rescue. The affinity with the story of Joseph in the pit runs through the poem, and "leper's lamp" may be equated either with the miner's lamp or with the isolation of a doomed man seeing the approach of death. A single interpretation is not really adequate.'

We need to know nothing of this to enjoy Watkins's *The Collier*. Poems have no need to lean too heavily on crutches of notes. But I think it should be remembered that even the simplest-sounding poem deserves the closest and most careful attention. Like the chameleon, a poem will often most wonderfully change while one is still looking at it. Peter Levi says that behind his poem *The fox-coloured pheasant enjoyed his peace* (page 36) stands the Bible story of Jacob wrestling with the Angel. We may also find in it something of the story of the hero Digenes, the half-breed border-fighter who wrestled with Death on a stone threshing-floor. But to many, the poem may be simply a startling account of a young sailor attacked at night while returning to his ship. To others, it may also be (as I believe it is) the story of one doubting man's search for a faith and a God.

Henry Treece's *Ballad* (page 40) seems much simpler, but is just as disturbing. It becomes even more exciting if we consider, as the poet once suggested, that the 'soldier' who stole the boy may never have been a soldier at all. He may be merely a vagabond in disguise : one who poisons with evil the minds of those younger than himself. So the ballad becomes a kind of parable of birth, life, and death itself. Shoals of such exciting hints and possibilities move beneath the surface of all poetry, and we have to fish for them ourselves.

I have tried to arrange this anthology so that it may be read straight through, the poems leading from one to another. The division into five parts is only based very roughly on subjects. The reader will soon discover that few poems have a *single*, simple idea, and that in fact most poetry has the magical quality of touching our lives on many points at the same time.

An anthology isn't of much value unless it leads to a wider reading of the work of the various poets. I hope that the details given in the list of contributors, (pages 113–123), will help here. In the end, I also hope that the reader may have the makings of the best anthology in the world: a personal and private one.

Poems are not clocks. If we take them to pieces and put them together again, they may still give no reason at all why they tick: nor should they. For it is important that all works of art should keep some of their secrets in order that they may go on giving out what the Spanish poet, Federico García Lorca, called *sonidos negros*, black sounds. These black sounds, he said, accompany all imaginative creations whether in words or paint, music or stone. Some poems are best read aloud. Others speak to the inward ear, and answer more clearly to silent reading. But however poems may differ on the surface, they have one important quality in common. They remain, as the painter Pablo Picasso has said of all art, weapons of war against brutality and darkness.

Charles Causley

ACKNOWLEDGMENTS

Grateful acknowledgments are made to the following for permission to reprint copyright material:

Dannie Abse and The Hutchinson Publishing Group for a poem from *Tenants of the House*

Kingsley Amis and Messrs Victor Gollancz Ltd for a poem from *A Case of Samples*

W. H. Auden and Messrs Faber & Faber Ltd for poems from *Collected Shorter Poems 1930–1944*

George Barker and Messrs Faber & Faber Ltd for a poem from *Collected Poems 1930–1955*

Frances Bellerby and Messrs Peter Davies Ltd for a poem from *The Brightening Cloud*

John Betjeman, Messrs John Murray Ltd and Houghton Mifflin for poems from *Collected Poems*

Thomas Blackburn and The Hand and Flower Press for a poem from *The Outer Darkness*

Mrs Mary Campbell and Messrs Curtis Brown Ltd for a poem by Roy Campbell from *Adamastor*, included in the *Collected Poems*, by arrangement with Faber & Faber Ltd

Charles Causley and Messrs Rupert Hart-Davis Ltd for poems from *Union Street* and *Johnny Alleluia*

Leonard Clark and Messrs Hutchinson for a poem from *The Saturday Book 18*

T. S. Eliot and Messrs Faber & Faber Ltd for poems from *Collected Poems 1909–1935*

Roy Fuller; Roy Fuller and Messrs André Deutsch Ltd for a poem from *Counterparts*

K. W. Gransden and Messrs Abelard-Schuman Ltd for a poem from *Any Day*

Robert Graves and International Authors N.V. for poems from *Collected Poems 1959* and *More Poems 1961*

Michael Hamburger

John Heath-Stubbs and Messrs Methuen & Co Ltd for poems from *A Charm against the Toothache*

Geoffrey Hill and Messrs André Deutsch Ltd for a poem from *For the Unfallen*

Kenneth Hopkins and Messrs Putnam & Co Ltd for a poem from *Forty-two Poems*

Ted Hughes and Messrs Faber & Faber Ltd for poems from *Lupercal*

Elizabeth Jennings and Messrs André Deutsch Ltd for a poem from *A Sense of the World*

James Kirkup and The Oxford University Press for a poem from *A Spring Journey*; James Kirkup and Grey Walls Press for a poem from *The Drowned Sailor*

At Grass by Philip Larkin is reprinted from *The Less Deceived* by permission of The Marvell Press

Peter Levi S.J., and Messrs André Deutsch Ltd for a poem from *The Gravel Ponds*

C. Day Lewis and Messrs Jonathan Cape Ltd with the Hogarth Press Ltd for a poem from *Collected Poems*

Christopher Logue and Messrs Hutchinson for a poem from *Songs*

Louis MacNeice and Messrs Faber & Faber Ltd for poems from *Collected Poems 1925–1948*

Messrs Faber & Faber Ltd for a poem by Edwin Muir from *Collected Poems 1921–1958*

Norman Nicholson and Messrs Faber & Faber Ltd for poems from *Rock Face* and *The Pot Geranium*

Ruth Pitter and The Cresset Press Ltd for poems from *Urania* and *The Ermine*

John Press and The Oxford University Press for a poem from *Uncertainties*

Sir Herbert Read and Messrs Faber & Faber Ltd for poems from *Collected Poems*

James Reeves and Messrs William Heinemann Ltd for poems from *Collected Poems 1929–1959*

Alan Ross and Messrs André Deutsch Ltd for poems from *Something of the Sea*

A. L. Rowse and Messrs Faber & Faber Ltd for a poem from *Poems of a Decade*: 1931–41

Jon Silkin and Messrs Chatto & Windus Ltd for a poem from *The Two Freedoms*

Edith Sitwell and Messrs Macmillan & Co Ltd for poems from *Collected Poems*

Sir Osbert Sitwell and Messrs MacMillan & Co. Ltd for a poem from *Wrack at Tidesend*; Sir Osbert Sitwell and Messrs Duckworth & Co Ltd for poems from *Selected Poems Old and New*

Stevie Smith and Messrs André Deutsch Ltd for poems from *Not Waving but Drowning*

Stephen Spender and Messrs Faber & Faber Ltd for a poem from *Collected Poems 1928–1953*

Messrs Methuen & Co Ltd for poems by L. A. G. Strong from *The Body's Imperfection*

Hal Summers

Messrs J. M. Dent & Sons Ltd for poems by Dylan Thomas from *Collected Poems 1934–1952*, and *Under Milk Wood*

R. S. Thomas and Messrs Rupert Hart-Davis Ltd for poems from *Song at the Year's Turning*

Anthony Thwaite

Henry Treece and Messrs Faber & Faber Ltd for a poem from *The Black Seasons*

John Wain and Messrs Routledge & Kegan Paul Ltd for a poem from *A Word Carved on a Sill*

Vernon Watkins and Messrs Faber & Faber Ltd for a poem from *Ballad of the Mari Lwyd*

Laurence Whistler and Messrs William Heinemann Ltd for a poem from *The World's Room*

David Wright

Andrew Young and Messrs Rupert Hart-Davis Ltd for poems from *The Collected Poems of Andrew Young*

1 Songs and Ballads

Johnnie Crack and Flossie Snail

from *Under Milk Wood*

Johnnie Crack and Flossie Snail
Kept their baby in a milking pail
Flossie Snail and Johnnie Crack
One would pull it out and one would put it back

O it's my turn now said Flossie Snail
To take the baby from the milking pail
And it's my turn now said Johnnie Crack
To smack it on the head and put it back

Johnnie Crack and Flossie Snail
Kept their baby in a milking pail
One would put it back and one would pull it out
And all it had to drink was ale and stout
For Johnnie Crack and Flossie Snail
Always used to say that stout and ale
Was *good* for a baby in a milking pail.

Dylan Thomas

The Lonely Scarecrow

My poor old bones – I've only two –
A broomshank and a broken stave.
My ragged gloves are a disgrace.
My one peg-foot is in the grave.

I wear the labourer's old clothes :
Coat, shirt, and trousers all undone.
I bear my cross upon a hill
In rain and shine, in snow and sun.

I cannot help the way I look.
My funny hat is full of hay.
– O, wild birds, come and nest in me !
Why do you always fly away ?

James Kirkup

Nipping Pussy's Feet in Fun

(This is not Kind)

Oh Mr Pussy-Cat
My, you are sweet!
How do you get about so much
On those tiny feet?
Nip, nip, miaou, miaou,
Tiny little feet,
Nip, nip pussy-cat
My, you are sweet!

Stevie Smith

Cat Asks Mouse Out

(But then Neither is This)

Mrs Mouse
Come out of your house
It is a fine sunny day
And I am waiting to play.

Bring the little ones too
And we can run to and fro.

Stevie Smith

And her mouth is sweet as a honey-flower cold
But her heart is heavy as bags of gold.

    The shadow-mice said,
    'We will line with down
    From those doves, our bed
    And our slippers and gown,

For everything comes to the shadows at last
If the spinning-wheel Time move slow or fast.'

Edith Sitwell

Madam Mouse trots

'*Dame Souris trotte grise dans le noir.*' – Verlaine

    Madame Mouse trots,
    Grey in the black night!
    Madame Mouse trots:
    Furred is the light.
    The elephant-trunks
    Trumpet from the sea . . .
    Grey in the black night
    The mouse trots free.
    Hoarse as a dog's bark
    The heavy leaves are furled . . .
    The cat's in his cradle,
    All's well with the world!

Edith Sitwell

Vain and Careless

Lady, lovely lady,
    Careless and gay!
Once, when a beggar called,
    She gave her child away.

The beggar took the baby,
    Wrapped it in a shawl –
'Bring him back,' the lady said,
    'Next time you call.'

Hard by lived a vain man,
    So vain and so proud
He would walk on stilts
    To be seen by the crowd,

Up above the chimney pots,
    Tall as a mast –
And all the people ran about
    Shouting till he passed.

'A splendid match surely,'
    Neighbours saw it plain,
'Although she is so careless,
    Although he is so vain.'

But the lady played bob-cherry,
    Did not see or care,
As the vain man went by her,
    Aloft in the air.

This gentle-born couple
    Lived and died apart –
Water will not mix with oil,
    Nor vain with careless heart.

Robert Graves

By the Firelight

If my baby have a squint,
I shall kill it, Mother!
Hush, thou mump-head, do not tell so,
Says her kindly mother.
Thou would love him dearly, dearly,
More than any other.

But my baby shall not squint,
Say he shall not, Mother?
No, my lovely, that he shall not,
Says her kindly mother.
He shall have straight starry eyes,
Cheeks so firm as apple pies,
He shall chuckle lovely-wise,
Louder, sweeter, rounder, fuller,
Better every way than any other!

L. A. G. Strong

Cradle Song

Hush, honey, hush –
The night won't be long;
Hush, honey, hush –
And I'll sing you a song.

Your cradle is rocking
A sweet lullaby;
The white stars are flocking
Across the sky.

Hush, honey, hush –
The night won't be long;
Hush, honey, hush –
And I'll sing you a song.

A little bird told me
He went to sleep
Ever so boldly
On a warm woolly sheep.

Hush, honey, hush –
The night won't be long;
Hush, honey, hush –
And I'll sing you a song.

Herbert Read

The Boy in the Barn

A little boy wandering alone in the night
Went in a barn all wrecked and decayed;
And the bats and the moths and the fluttering things
Flew in his face and made him afraid.

So he fell on the floor and buried his head,
And his lantern fell down at his feet;
And he heard as he lay on the sweet-smelling hay
His little heart beat, beat, beat . . .

O little boy lift your light aloft
And the bats will scamper away;
And the big brown moths will kiss the flame
And flutter down dead on the sweet-smelling hay.

Herbert Read

Out of School

Four o'clock strikes,
There's a rising hum,
Then the doors fly open,
The children come.

With a wild cat-call
And a hop-scotch hop
And a bouncing ball
And a whirling top,

Grazing of knees,
A hair-pull and a slap,
A hitched up satchel,
A pulled down cap,

Bully boys reeling off,
Hurt ones squealing off,
Aviators wheeling off,
Mousy ones stealing off,

Woollen gloves for chilblains,
Cotton rags for snufflers,
Pigtails, coat-tails,
Tails of mufflers,

Machine gun cries,
A kennelful of snarlings,
A hurricane of leaves,
A treeful of starlings,

Thinning away now
By some and some,
Thinning away, away,
All gone home.

Hal Summers

Henry and Mary

Henry was a young king,
    Mary was his queen;
He gave her a snowdrop
    On a stalk of green.

Then all for his kindness
    And for all his care,
She gave him a new-laid egg
    In the garden there.

'Love, can you sing?'
            'I cannot sing.'
  'Or tell a tale?'
             'Not one I know.'
'Then let us play at queen and king
    As down the garden walks we go.'

Robert Graves

Nursery Rhyme of Innocence and Experience

I had a silver penny
    And an apricot tree
And I said to the sailor
    On the white quay

'Sailor O sailor
    Will you bring me
If I give you my penny
    And my apricot tree

A fez from Algeria
    An Arab drum to beat
A little gilt sword
    And a parakeet?'

And he smiled and he kissed me
    As strong as death
And I saw his red tongue
    And I felt his sweet breath

'You may keep your penny
    And your apricot tree
And I'll bring your presents
    Back from sea.'

O the ship dipped down
    On the rim of the sky
And I waited while three
    Long summers went by

Then one steel morning
    On the white quay
I saw a grey ship
    Come in from sea

Slowly she came
    Across the bay

For her flashing rigging
  Was shot away

All round her wake
  The seabirds cried
And flew in and out
  Of the hole in her side

Slowly she came
  In the path of the sun
And I heard the sound
  Of a distant gun

And a stranger came running
  Up to me
From the deck of the ship
  And he said, said he

'*O are you the boy*
  Who would wait on the quay
With the silver penny
  And the apricot tree?

I've a plum-coloured fez
  And a drum for thee
And a sword and a parakeet
  From over the sea.'

'O where is the sailor
  With bold red hair?
And what is that volley
  On the bright air?

O where are the other
  Girls and boys?
And why have you brought me
  Children's toys?'

                Charles Causley

Wild Wilbur

Wild Wilbur paces by the caves
his limbs are long his smile is wide
his hands are dangling side to side
his eyes are fixed upon the waves.

The birds sing in his healthy ears
the waves spill round his anklesocks
sometimes he spits upon the rocks
sometimes he picks his nose with tears.

Look how he sighs out of his chest
look how his feet sail on the ground
there is no need to make a sound
when Wilbur smiles all is at rest.

Below his sailorcollar and
below his modest undervest
below each slight selfcentred breast
below his navel filled with sand

the bright tattooings intertwine
the dragons and the serpents rise
from his adjacent bevelled thighs
come smells of swimming, cups of brine.

He knows the value of his size
he finds the stillness comforting
he wanders like a trackless thing
upon a world too small for eyes.

James Kirkup

Shanty

Shanty of the singing sailor
    striking up the rock of dawn,
all the day, there I lay,
    in the Bay of Biscay, I
heard the brassy voice of ocean
    from drowned Tuscorora come,

and the larynx of the wind
    chorded with the yell of gull,
all the day, there I lay,
    in the Bay of Biscay, I
heard the empty well of ocean,
    the surrender of the sun

drowned below the risen star
    . peal upon the rolling swell,
all the day, there I lay,
    in the Bay of Biscay, I
heard the salt tongue of the sailor
    climb the castle of the sun.

David Wright

The Goole Captain

One day as I walked by Crocodile Mansions
I met a young woman, sea-green were her eyes,
And she was loud weeping by the banks of the Humber,
O, bitter the sound of her sobs and her sighs.

I asked this young woman why she was sore weeping,
'Pray, tell me,' I said, 'why you grieve by the tide?'
And when I had put my arm tightly around her,
In a voice like a sea bird she sadly replied,

'I was born, sir, at Wetwang, but I left the East Riding,
With the cows and the sheep as a girl I would roam,
And if I were back with my father and brothers
I'd ne'er leave again the sweet fields of my home.'

So I led her so gently past Crocodile Mansions,
And I took her so gently by the banks of the Humber,
She gave herself freely, her eyes and her kisses,
And I gave her a gold ring and a necklet of amber.

When we parted at stardown no more was she weeping,
But the very next morning as I sailed out with the tide,
She waved to me gaily as we hove round the headland
And I yearned for her beauty to be by my side.

O, I sailed for a year and a day to the Indies
And I came back to England one green day in spring
But I had forgotten the girl with the green eyes,
The necklet of amber, the little gold ring.

But as I was strolling down the Land of Green Ginger
While our ship loaded up with a cargo for Poole,
The people they looked at me strangely and whispered,
'O, beware of the faithless young captain from Goole.'

So I went off at once to Crocodile Mansions
To look for my dear love with sea-green eyes,
But no-one would tell me or answer my questions,
O, bitter my heart then and empty my sighs.

Then I met in 'The Dragon' a drunken old sailor
Who told me he'd seen her with a necklet of amber,
A little gold ring and her eyes green and staring
Floating far out to sea by the banks of the Humber.

And I walked for the last time by Crocodile Mansions,
My heart was so full I shed never a tear
O, I looked at the sea and I looked at the Humber
And in every green wave were the eyes of my dear.

Leonard Clark

Land of Green Ginger is the name of a street in Hull, and Wet-
wang is a village in the East Riding of Yorkshire.

The fox-coloured pheasant enjoyed his peace

The fox-coloured pheasant enjoyed his peace,
there were no labourers in the wheat,
dogs were stretched out at ease,
the empty road echoed my feet.

It was the time for owls' voices,
trees were dripping dark like rain,
and sheep made night-time noises
as I went down the hill lane.

In the streets of the still town
I met a man in the lamplight,
he stood in the alley that led down
to the harbour and the sea out of sight.

Who do you want? he asked me,
Who are you looking for in this place?
The houses echoed us emptily
and the lamp shone on his face.

Does your girl live here?
(There were no girls or sailors about.)
I have no girl anywhere,
I want a ship putting out.

He stood under the lamplight
and I stepped up close to him,
his eyes burned like fires at night
and the lamp seemed dim.

He came closer up and pressed
his crooked knee to my knee,
and his chest to my chest,
and held my shoulders and wrestled with me.

It was the middle time of night
with five hours to run till day,
but the sky was crimson and bright
before he stood out of my way.

I ran past as quick as I could
and the wet stones rang loudly
along the wharf where the ships stood
and the sea lifting proudly.

Peter Levi S.J.

Glass Falling

The glass is going down. The sun
Is going down. The forecasts say
It will be warm, with frequent showers.
We ramble down the showery hours
And amble up and down the day.
Mary will wear her black goloshes
And splash the puddles on the town;
And soon on fleets of macintoshes
The rain is coming down, the frown
Is coming down of heaven showing
A wet night coming, the glass is going
Down, the sun is going down.

Louis MacNeice

Death by Water (Part *IV* of *The Waste Land*)

Phlebas the Phœnician, a fortnight dead,
Forgot the cry of gulls, and the deep sea swell
And the profit and loss.
                                    A current under sea
Picked his bones in whispers. As he rose and fell
He passed the stages of his age and youth
Entering the whirlpool.
                                    Gentile or Jew
O you who turn the wheel and look to windward,
Consider Phlebas, who was once handsome and tall as you.

T. S. Eliot

Jonah

He stands in rags upon the heaving prow
Stiff as the mast behind him, and the rain
Channels the filthy wrinkles of his brow,
Driving to Nineveh. Beneath his brain
That severs their bruised water like a keel,
Yeasty with spirit, mount the rebel streams
And scatter on his lips their yellow foam.

Then that extreme volition he would flee
Pours downward its green fury, snaps his bands,
As, final mutiny, the Prophet's hands
Rise up and fling him to the hungry sea.

How gently then the mercy takes this child
Into a silence, turns, and with her choice
Swims through the mild embraces of the flood
To that great city hungry for his voice.

Thomas Blackburn

38

Apples and Water

Dust in a cloud, blinding weather,
    Drums that rattle and roar!
A mother and daughter stood together
    By their cottage door.

'Mother, the heavens are bright like brass,
    The dust is shaken high,
With labouring breath the soldiers pass,
    Their lips are cracked and dry.

'Mother, I'll throw them apples down,
    I'll fetch them cups of water.'
The mother turned with an angry frown,
    Holding back her daughter.

'But, mother, see, they faint with thirst,
    They march away to war.'
'Ay, daughter, these are not the first
    And there will come yet more.

'There is no water can supply them
    In western streams that flow;
There is no fruit can satisfy them
    On orchard-trees that grow.

'Once in my youth I gave, poor fool,
    A soldier apples and water;
And may I die before you cool
    Such drouth as his, my daughter.'

Robert Graves

39

Ballad

Oh come, my joy, my soldier boy,
With your golden buttons, your scarlet coat,
Oh let me play with your twinkling sword
And sail away in your wonderful boat!

The soldier came and took the boy.
Together they marched the dusty roads.
Instead of war, they sang at Fairs,
And mended old chairs with river reeds.

The boy put on a little black patch
And learned to sing on a tearful note;
The soldier sold his twinkling sword
To buy a crutch and a jet-black flute.

And when the summer sun rode high
They laughed the length of the shining day;
But when the robin stood in the hedge
The little lad's courage drained away.

Oh soldier, my soldier, take me home
To the nut-brown cottage under the hill.
My mother is waiting, I'm certain sure;
She's far too old to draw at the well!

As snowflakes fell the boy spoke so,
For twenty years, ah twenty years;
But a look in the soldier's eyes said no,
And the roads of England were wet with tears.

One morning, waking on the moors,
The lad laughed loud at the corpse by his side.
He buried the soldier under a stone,
But kept the flute to soothe his pride.

The days dragged on and he came to a town,
Where he got a red jacket for chopping wood;
And meeting a madman by the way,
He bartered the flute for a twinkling sword.

And so he walked the width of the land
With a warlike air and a jaunty word,
Looking out for a likely lad,
With the head of a fool and the heart of a bard.

Henry Treece

O what is that sound which so thrills the ear

O what is that sound which so thrills the ear
    Down in the valley drumming, drumming?
Only the scarlet soldiers, dear,
    The soldiers coming.

O what is that light I see flashing so clear
    Over the distance brightly, brightly?
Only the sun on their weapons, dear,
    As they step lightly.

O what are they doing with all that gear,
    What are they doing this morning, this morning?
Only their usual manœuvres, dear,
    Or perhaps a warning.

O why have they left the road down there,
    Why are they suddenly wheeling, wheeling?
Perhaps a change in their orders, dear.
    Why are you kneeling?

O haven't they stopped for the doctor's care,
    Haven't they reined their horses, their horses?
Why, they are none of them wounded, dear,
    None of these forces.

O is it the parson they want, with white hair,
    Is it the parson, is it, is it?
No, they are passing his gateway, dear,
    Without a visit.

O it must be the farmer who lives so near.
    It must be the farmer so cunning, so cunning?
They have passed the farmyard already, dear,
    And now they are running.

O where are you going? Stay with me here!
    Were the vows you swore deceiving, deceiving?
No, I promised to love you, dear,
    But I must be leaving.

O it's broken the lock and splintered the door,
    O it's the gate where they're turning, turning;
Their boots are heavy on the floor
    And their eyes are burning.

W. H. Auden

Over the heather the wet wind blows

Over the heather the wet wind blows,
I've lice in my tunic and a cold in my nose.

The rain comes pattering out of the sky,
I'm a Wall soldier, I don't know why.

The mist creeps over the hard grey stone,
My girl's in Tungria; I sleep alone.

Aulus goes hanging around her place,
I don't like his manners, I don't like his face.

Piso's a Christian, he worships a fish;
There'd be no kissing if he had his wish.

She gave me a ring but I diced it away,
I want my girl and I want my pay.

When I'm a veteran with only one eye
I shall do nothing but look at the sky.

W. H. Auden

2 The Other World

Allie

Allie, call the birds in,
   The birds from the sky!
Allie calls, Allie sings,
   Down they all fly:
First there came
Two white doves,
   Then a sparrow from his nest,
Then a clucking bantam hen,
   Then a robin red-breast.

Allie, call the beasts in,
   The beasts, every one!
Allie calls, Allie sings,
   In they all run:
First there came
Two black lambs,
   Then a grunting Berkshire sow,
Then a dog without a tail,
   Then a red and white cow.

Allie, call the fish up,
   The fish from the stream!
Allie calls, Allie sings,
   Up they all swim:
First there came
Two gold fish,
   A minnow and a miller's thumb,
Then a school of little trout,
   Then the twisting eels come.

Allie, call the children,
   Call them from the green!
Allie calls, Allie sings,
   Soon they run in:

First there came
Tom and Madge,
       Kate and I who'll not forget
How we played by the water's edge
       Till the April sun set.

Robert Graves

An old man sat in a waterfall

An old man sat in a waterfall
       And the water dripped through his hair;
His voice was green as a sea-pie's call:
'Come weeds, and turf my skull,
For my hair is loosed by the bite of the beck –
       Soon my head will be bare;
       I'll have no pride at all.

'Come wagtail, water-ousel sing
       And bubble in my throat;
Come water-rat skulk in my breast,
My flesh shall be your winter coat;
Come water-hen and make your nest
       In hollows of my ribs;
There you'll find a place to play,
For life has rotted my heart away.'

The old man sat in the waterfall
And the water turned his skin to bone.
Stalactites hung from his chin like a beard;
       His shoulders were shelled with stone.
And leaves in autumn drop from tall
Arthritic thorn-trees by the limestone wall
On the old stone man in the waterfall.

Norman Nicholson

In this poem, the poet asks us to remember that if objects are immersed long enough in some limestone springs, they become calcified – that is, changed into lime. So does the Old Man.

The Stone Gentleman

Let us move the stone gentleman to the toadstool wood:
Too long has he disapproved in our market-place.
Within the manifold stone creases of his frock-coat
    Let the woodlouse harbour and thrive.

Let the hamadryads wreath him with bryony,
The scrolled fern-fronds greenly fantasticate,
And sappy etiolations cluster damply
    About the paternal knee.

Them the abrupt, blank eyes will not offend.
The civic brow and raised, suppressive hand
Unchallenged and without affront shall manage
    The republic of tall spiders.

James Reeves

Hamadryads are wood-nymphs who spend their lives inside trees,
and also die there.

The Shepherd's Hut

The smear of blue peat smoke
That staggered on the wind and broke,
The only sign of life,
Where was the shepherd's wife,
Who left those flapping clothes to dry,
Taking no thought for her family?
For, as they bellied out
And limbs took shape and waved about,
I thought, She little knows
That ghosts are trying on her children's clothes.

Andrew Young

Tom

The farmhand Tom, with his apple and turnip face,
Grumbles, grins and groans through the long summer hours,
Reviles St Martin, by whose grace
Thus he must plod through the poppies and cornflowers.
Night is a stretch of dead and drear slumber,
Then up again, and again he must lumber
Into his clothes and away through the park,
Carrying pails,   Must wade through the dark.
Till even the comforting darkness fails,
Tousled and blinking,
Clanking and clinking,
A very robust
Traditional ghost :
    For clanking and lank
    The Armoured Knight
    Rides down the dank
    Shadows in flight;
    Grass stiff with frost
    Shows grey as steel
    As the Conquering Ghost
    Clanks down the hill.
        Now the first cock crows,
        Impudent, frightened, through the dark;
        Then a cold wind blows,
    And that whining dog, Dawn, begins to bark.
Then the Knight in Armour
Passes away,
As the growing clamour
Proclaims, 'It is Day.'
The trees grow taller,
The gate is shut.
The Knight grows smaller,   Goes smaller,   And out.

Osbert Sitwell

49

Kitchen Song

Grey as a guinea-fowl is the rain
Squawking down from the boughs again.
    'Anne, Anne,
      Go fill the pail,'
Said the old witch who sat on the rail.
'Though there is a hole in the bucket,
Anne, Anne,
It will fill my pocket;
The water-drops when they cross my doors
Will turn to guineas and gold moidores . . .
The well-water hops across the floors;
Whimpering, 'Anne' it cries, implores,
And the guinea-fowl-plumaged rain,
Squawking down from the boughs again,
Cried, 'Anne, Anne, go fill the bucket,
There is a hole in the witch's pocket –
And the water-drops like gold moidores,
Obedient girl, will surely be yours.
So, Anne, Anne,
Go fill the pail
Of the old witch who sits on the rail!'

Edith Sitwell

The Two Witches

O, sixteen hundred and ninety one,
Never was year so well begun,
Backsy-forsy and inside-out,
The best of all years to ballad about.

On the first fine day of January
I ran to my sweetheart Margery
And tossed her over the roof so far
That down she fell like a shooting star.

But when we two had frolicked and kissed
She clapped her fingers about my wrist
And tossed me over the chimney stack,
And danced on me till my bones did crack.

Then, when she had laboured to ease my pain,
We sat by the stile of Robin's Lane,
She in a hare and I in a toad
And puffed at the clouds till merry they glowed.

We spelled our loves until close of day.
I wished her good-night and walked away,
But she put out a tongue that was long and red
And swallowed me down like a crumb of bread.

Robert Graves

Notice how the year 1691 reads the same upside-down: in fact,
as Robert Graves says:

Backsy-forsy and inside-out,
The best of all years to ballad about.

51

La Tour du Sorcier

Whence comes the crooked wind
    To set your steeple, witch's hat, a-turning;
Whence comes the light, that rind
    Of fire, to set each stone a-burning;
From what strange mountain in the whiteness lone
Of moon-range comes that wind's quiet moan?

Why is the slanting turret bare,
    Why grow the weeds so rank;
Why are sly windows peeping there,
    And the shadows so lank?
Whence comes your height, seeming higher than your neighbour,
Whence comes your wraith-like whiteness in the moon's white labour?

Crouching, a shadow lingers, bat-wing'd, at your door,
    Looking down first at the herbs and then up at the stars.
Arching its back, a black cat scampers over the floor,
    In the dark chamber where blossom the stars between bars.

Ancient, I ask you, is it the stars you cull
    When you're in darkness, as here with the lank herbs below;
Where is the Archer to-night, and the Twins and the Bull?
    Why are the great tides sweeping us to and fro?

Osbert Sitwell

The Archer, the Twins, and the Bull are all groups of stars being
gathered by the Wizard in his Tower.

A Charm Against the Toothache

Venerable Mother Toothache
Climb down from the white battlements,
Stop twisting in your yellow fingers
The fourfold rope of nerves;
And to-morrow I will give you a tot òf whisky
To hold in your cupped hands,
A garland of anise-flowers,
And three cloves like nails.

And tell the attendant gnomes
It is time to knock off now,
To shoulder their little pick-axes,
Their cold-chisels and drills.
And you may mount by a silver ladder
Into the sky, to grind
In the cracked polished mortar
Of the hollow moon.

By the lapse of warm waters,
And the poppies nodding like red coals,
The paths on the granite mountains,
And the plantation òf my dreams.

John Heath-Stubbs

The Enchanted Knight

Lulled by La Belle Dame Sans Merci he lies
    In the bare wood below the blackening hill.
The plough drives nearer now, the shadow flies
    Past him across the plain, but he lies still.

Long since the rust its gardens here has planned,
    Flowering his armour like an autumn field.
From his sharp breast-plate to his iron hand
    A spider's web is stretched, a phantom shield.

When footsteps pound the turf beside his ear
    Armies pass through his dream in endless line,
And one by one his ancient friends appear;
    They pass all day, but he can make no sign.

When a bird cries within the silent grove
    The long-lost voice goes by, he makes to rise
And follow, but his cold limbs never move,
    And on the turf unstirred his shadow lies.

But if a withered leaf should drift
    Across his face and rest, the dread drops start
Chill on his forehead. Now he tries to lift
    The insulting weight that stays and breaks his heart.

Edwin Muir

If you want to learn more of Edwin Muir's *Enchanted Knight* read *La Belle Dame Sans Merci*, a ballad by John Keats (1795–1821). This mysterious tale tells of how the pitiless lady, 'a faery's child', first puts the knight-at-arms under her spell, lures him at last to the cold hill's side, and leaves him there:

> *O, what can ail thee, knight-at-arms,*
>   *Alone and palely loitering?*
> *The sedge has wither'd from the lake*
>   *And no birds sing.*

How many miles to Mylor?

How many miles to Mylor
    By frost and candle-light:
How long before I arrive there,
    This mild December night?

As I mounted the hill to Mylor
    Through the thick woods of Carclew,
A clock struck the three-quarters,
    And suddenly a cock crew.

At the cross-roads on the hill-top
    The snow lay on the ground,
In the quick air and the stillness,
    No movement and no sound.

'How is it?' said a voice from the bushes
    Beneath the rowan-tree;
'Who is it?' my mouth re-echoed,
    My heart went out of me.

I cannot tell what queerness
    There lay around Carclew:
Nor whatever stirred in the hedges
    When an owl replied 'Who-whoo?'

A lamp in a lone cottage,
    A face in a window-frame,
Above the snow a wicket:
    A house without a name.

How many miles to Mylor
  This dark December night :
And shall I ever arrive there   '
  By frost or candle-light?

A. L. Rowse

Mylor is a tiny village at the head of Mylor Creek, Cornwall.

Lowery Cot

For Robert Graves

This is the house where Jesse White
Run staring in one misty night,
And said he seed the Holy Ghost
Out to Lowery finger-post.

Said It rised up like a cloud
Muttering to Itself out loud,
And stood tremendous on the hill
While all the breathing world was still.

They put en shivering to bed,
And in three days the man was dead.
Gert solemn visions such as they
Be overstrong for mortal clay.

L. A. G. Strong

3

Carnival of Animals

The Rescue

The boy climbed up into the tree.
The tree rocked. So did he.
He was trying to rescue a cat,
A cushion of a cat, from where it sat
In a high crutch of branches, mewing
As though to say to him, 'Nothing doing,'
Whenever he shouted, 'Come on, come down.'
So up he climbed, and the whole town
Lay at his feet, round him the leaves
Fluttered like a lady's sleeves,
And the cat sat, and the wind blew so
That he would have flown had he let go.
At last he was high enough to scoop
That fat white cushion or nincompoop
And tuck her under his arm and turn
To go down –
                    But oh! he began to learn
How high he was, how hard it would be,
Having come up with four limbs, to go down with three.
His heart-beats knocked as he tried to think:
He would put the cat in a lower chink –
She appealed to him with a cry of alarm
And put her eighteen claws in his arm.
So he stayed looking down for a minute or so,
To the good ground so far below.
When the minute began he saw it was hard;
When it ended he couldn't move a yard.
So there he was stuck, in the failing light
And the wind rising with the coming of the night.

His father! He shouted for all he was worth.
His father came nearer: 'What on earth – ?'

'I've got the cat up here but I'm stuck.'
'Hold on . . . ladder . . .', he heard. O luck!
How lovely behind the branches tossing
The globes at the pedestrian crossing
And the big fluorescent lamps glowed
Mauve-green on the main road.
But his father didn't come back, didn't come;
His little fingers were going numb.
The cat licked them as though to say
'Are you feeling cold? I'm O.K.'
He wanted to cry, he would count ten first,
But just as he was ready to burst
A torch came and his father and mother
And a ladder and the dog and his younger brother.
Up on a big branch stood his father,
His mother came to the top of the ladder,
His brother stood on a lower rung,
The dog sat still and put out its tongue.
From one to the other the cat was handed
And afterwards she was reprimanded.
After that it was easy, though the wind blew :
The parents came down, the boy came too
From the ladder, the lower branch and the upper
And all of them went indoors to supper,
And the tree rocked, and the moon sat
In the high branches like a white cat.

Hal Summers

Little Fable

The mouse like halting clockwork, in the light
A shade of biscuit, curved towards the right

And hid behind the gas-stove, peeping out
A sickly moment with its pencil snout.

Its run was blocked to keep it in the wall
But at the time it was not there at all.

The food is covered and a penny trap,
Being bought, is baited with a bacon scrap.

Its back is guillotined and seen to be
Grey and not brown, its feet formed properly.

Thus the obscene becomes pathetic and
What mind had feared is stroked by hand.

Roy Fuller

Nino, the Wonder Dog

A dog emerges from the flies
    Balanced upon a ball.
Our entertainment is the fear
    Or hope the dog will fall.

It comes and goes on larger spheres,
    And then walks on and halts
In the centre of the stage and turns
    Two or three somersaults.

The curtains descend upon the act.
    After a proper pause
The dog comes out between them to
    Receive its last applause.

Most mouths are set in pitying smiles,
　　Few eyes are free from rheum :
The sensitive are filled with thoughts
　　Of death and love and doom.

No doubt behind this ugly dog,
　　Frail, fairly small, and white,
Stands some beneficent protector,
　　Some life outside the night.

But this is not apparent as
　　It goes, in the glare alone,
Through what it must to serve absurd-
　　ities beyond its own.

Roy Fuller

Horses

The long whip lingers,
Toys with the sawdust;
The horses amble
On a disc of dreams.

The drumsticks flower
In pink percussion
To mix with the metal
Petals of brass.

The needle runs
In narrower circles;
The long whip leaps
And leads them inward.

Piebald horses
And ribald music
Circle around
A spangled lady.

Louis MacNeice

At Grass

The eye can hardly pick them out
From the cold shade they shelter in,
Till wind distresses tail and mane;
Then one crops grass, and moves about
– The other seeming to look on –
And stands anonymous again.

Yet fifteen years ago, perhaps
Two dozen distances sufficed
To fable them : faint afternoons
Of Cups and Stakes and Handicaps,
Whereby their names were artificed
To inlay faded, classic Junes –

Silks at the start : against the sky
Numbers and parasols : outside,
Squadrons of empty cars, and heat,
And littered grass : then the long cry
Hanging unhushed till it subside
To stop-press columns on the street.

Do memories plague their ears like flies?
They shake their heads. Dusk brims the shadows.
Summer by summer all stole away,
The starting-gates, the crowds and cries –
All but the unmolesting meadows.
Almanacked, their names live; they

Have slipped their names, and stand at ease,
Or gallop for what must be joy,
And not a field-glass sees them home,
Or curious stop-watch prophesies :
Only the groom, and the groom's boy,
With bridles in the evening come.

Philip Larkin

The silks are the jockeys' coloured blouses.

Man and Cows

I stood aside to let the cows
Swing past me with their wrinkled brows,
Bowing their heads as they went by
As to a woodland deity
To whom they turned mute eyes
To save them from the plaguing god of flies.

And I too cursed Beelzebub,
Watching them stop to rub
A bulging side or bony haunch
Against a trunk or pointing branch
And lift a tufted tail
To thresh the air with its soft flail.

They stumbled heavily down the slope,
As Hethor led them or the hope
Of the lush meadow-grass,
While I remained, thinking it was
Strange that we both were held divine,
In Egypt these, man once in Palestine.

Andrew Young

Hedgehog

Twitching the leaves just where the drainpipe clogs
In ivy leaves and mud, a purposeful
Creature at night about its business. Dogs
Fear his stiff seriousness. He chews away

At beetles, worms, slugs, frogs. Can kill a hen
With one snap of his jaws, can taunt a snake
To death on muscled spines. Old countrymen
Tell tales of hedgehogs sucking a cow dry.

But this one, cramped by houses, fences, walls,
Must have slept here all winter in that heap
Of compost, or have inched by intervals
Through tidy gardens to this ivy bed.

And here, dim-eyed, but ears so sensitive
A voice within the house can make him freeze,
He scuffs the edge of danger; yet can live
Happily in our nights and absences.

A country creature, wary, quiet and shrewd,
He takes the milk we give him, when we're gone.
At night, our slamming voices must seem crude
To one who sits and waits for silences.

Anthony Thwaite

The hedgehog lived in Anthony Thwaite's back garden, not far from London. Thwaite was fascinated by the strangeness of how wild animals still go on making their homes in man-made places, even though hemmed in by brick and stone.

Bullfrog

With their lithe long strong legs
Some frogs are able
To thump upon double-
Bass strings though pond-water deadens and clogs.

But you, bullfrog, you pump out
Whole fogs full of horn – a threat
As of a liner looming. True
That, first hearing you
Disgorging your gouts of darkness like a wounded god,
Not utterly fantastical I expected
(As in some antique tale depicted)
A broken-down bull up to its belly in mud,
Sucking black swamp up, belching out black cloud

And a squall of gudgeon and lilies.
                                    A surprise.
To see you, a boy's prize,
No bigger than a rat – all dumb silence
In your little old woman hands.

Ted Hughes

Ted Hughes has worked in America, and while there he was
deeply impressed by the noise of the bullfrog. 'It has to be heard
to be believed,' he says. 'My poem exaggerates nothing.'

An Otter

(Part I)

Underwater eyes, an eel's
Oil of water body, neither fish nor beast is the otter :
   Four-legged yet water-gifted, to outfish fish;
     With webbed feet and long ruddering tail
     And a round head like an old tomcat.

   Brings the legend of himself
From before wars or burials, in spite of hounds and vermin-poles;
   Does not take root like the badger. Wanders, cries;
     Gallops along land he no longer belongs to;
     Re-enters the water by melting.

   Of neither water nor land. Seeking
Some world lost when first he dived, that he cannot come at since,
   Takes his changed body into the holes of lakes;
     As if blind, cleaves the stream's push till he licks
     The pebbles of the source; from sea

   To sea crosses in three nights
Like a king in hiding. Crying to the old shape of the starlit land,
   Over sunken farms where the bats go round,
     Without answer. Till light and birdsong come
     Walloping up roads with the milk wagon.

Ted Hughes

The Bat

Lightless, unholy, eldritch thing,
Whose murky and erratic wing
Swoops so sickenly, and whose
Aspect to the female Muse
Is a demon's, made of stuff
Like tattered, sooty waterproof,
Looking dirty, clammy, cold.

Wicked, poisonous, and old;
I have maligned thee! . . . for the Cat
Lately caught a little bat,
Seized it softly, bore it in.
On the carpet, dark as sin
In the lamplight, painfully
It limped about, and could not fly.

Even fear must yield to love,
And pity makes the depths to move.
Though sick with horror, I must stoop,
Grasp it gently, take it up,
And carry it, and place it where
It could resume the twilight air.

Strange revelation! warm as milk,
Clean as a flower, smooth as silk!
O what a piteous face appears,
What great fine thin translucent ears!
What chestnut down and crapy wings,
Finer than any lady's things –
And O a little one that clings!

Warm, clean, and lovely, though not fair,
And burdened with a mother's care;
Go hunt the hurtful fly, and bear
My blessing to your kind in air.

Ruth Pitter

The Viper

Barefoot I went and made no sound;
The earth was hot beneath:
The air was quivering around,
The circling kestrel eyed the ground
And hung above the heath.

There in the pathway stretched along
The lovely serpent lay:
She reared not up the heath among,
She bowed her head, she sheathed her tongue,
And shining stole away.

Fair was the brave embroidered dress,
Fairer the gold eyes shone:
Loving her not, yet did I bless
The fallen angel's comeliness;
And gazed when she had gone.

Ruth Pitter

Good Taste

Travelling, a man met a tiger, so . . .
He ran. The tiger ran after him
Thinking: How fast I run . . . But

The road thought: How long I am . . . Then,
They came to a cliff, yes, the man
Grabbed at an ash root and swung down

Over its edge. Above his knuckles, the tiger.
At the foot of the cliff, its mate. Two mice,
One black, one white, began to gnaw the root.

And by the traveller's head grew one
Juicy strawberry, so . . . hugging the root
The man reached out and plucked the fruit.

How sweet it tasted!

Christopher Logue

Death of a Bird

After those first days
When we had placed him in his iron cage
And made a space for him
From such

Outrageous cage of wire,
Long and shallow, where the sunlight fell
Through the air, onto him;
After

He had been fed for three days
Suddenly, in that sunlight before noon
He was dead with no
Pretence.

He did not say goodbye
He did not say thankyou, but he died then
Lying flat on the rigid
Wires

Of his cage, his gold
Beak shut tight, which once in hunger had
Opened as a trap
And then

Swiftly closed again,
Swallowing quickly what I had given him;
How can I say I am sorry
He died.

Seeing him lie there dead,
Death's friend with death, I was angry he
Had gone without pretext or warning,
With no

Suggestion first he should go,
Since I had fed him, then put wires round him
Bade him hop across
The bars of my hands.

I asked him only that
He should desire his life. He had become
Of us a black friend with
A gold mouth

Shrilly singing through
The heat. The labour of the black bird! I
Cannot understand why
He is dead.

I bury him familiarly.
His heritage is a small brown garden.
Something is added to the everlasting earth;
From my mind a space is taken away.

Jon Silkin

Dead and Gone

This blackbird stared at us six feet away,
Set in a hedge, its poise at once too pure,
Too sure and still to be a real bird :
We, in the room, through glass, watched it and still
Without fear, in the hedge, it stood and watched us too.

Caught in the moment of alighting, died.

Caught by no cat : I looked for blood, or mess
Of feathers disarrayed. And certainly no hawk.
Here – where the suburbs cheat a violent death
By natural tooth or claw – it gripped a twig
With each long plucking claw, fanned out its wings,
Threw back its head and beak.

                                    Only its eyes,
Glazed to opaqueness, said that something died.

My daughter, three years old, whose practical eyes
See spiders, flies and ladybirds 'asleep',
Who lays out berries for them when they wake,
Asked me what I would do. 'I'll bury it –
Put it in a hole.' 'And will it hide like me?'

No need, though, for such ceremony as this.
We left the bird – memento, incident
Strange in the level course of things – all night.
In the morning, nothing. The leaves ruffled where
It took its stance, one of them crumpled by
The gripping claw. A hole where nothing was
Before or after. Buried in blank air.

This small death, vanishing from time and place,
Left this small gap, a childish question asked
And never answered. 'Why did the bird go?'
Well, common-sense would answer with a cat
Prowling from neighbouring gardens. Maybe so.
And yet, dead of old age or whatever else,
Those wings, heraldic, that full throat thrust back,
Those blind white eyes, announced some hiding-place,
Shared with the spider, ladybird and fly,
With child and man. And could not tell us why.

Anthony Thwaite

The blackbird (like the hedgehog in the poem on page 64) was
a real one: it died in the poet's front garden. Anthony Thwaite
has three small daughters, and the three-year-old was at that
time very fond of hiding in holes and all sorts of shut-in places.
She thought that when the blackbird came to be buried, it would
rather enjoy this kind of shut-in game too.

Flight

By day, the returning terror of swifts, the scream
Of the loop over leaf, the power-dive on to the thatch;
And the robin whose vivid gift is a tongue of flame
To startle the stone at your foot into lyrical speech.
By night, the approach of the bat, neurotic and odd,
A flicker of bony fingers here and there;
And the cool owl swimming in the blinded wood,
A big moth saying nothing in grey air.

By day, the shuttle of colour, speed that belongs
To the shadow that drops like a stone, the jewel that soars.
By night, the suspicion, the mere innuendo of wings,
The hint of a fugitive shadow across the stars.

By day, *Jubilate* of saints in the heart of the holly.
By night, the cry of the lost in the luminous valley.

Laurence Whistler

Cape Ann

O quick quick quick, quick hear the song-sparrow,
Swamp-sparrow, fox-sparrow, vesper-sparrow
At dawn and dusk. Follow the dance
Of the goldfinch at noon. Leave to chance
The Blackburnian warbler, the shy one. Hail
With shrill whistle the note of the quail, the bob-white
Dodging by bay-bush. Follow the feet
Of the walker, the water-thrush. Follow the flight
Of the dancing arrow, the purple martin. Greet
In silence the bullbat. All are delectable. Sweet sweet sweet
But resign this land at the end, resign it
To its true owner, the tough one, the sea-gull.
The palaver is finished.

T. S. Eliot

Aubade: Dick, the Donkey-boy

1

Tall, with tow-hair, the texture of hide,
Dick must saddle his drove, jump and ride,
Leading through the donkey-coloured dawn,
    In a sharp staccato clatter,
        A pattern, a patter
Of hooves hitting the road,

Down the donkey-coloured hill,
By the donkey-coloured vale,
To the sea's golden lawn,
    New stripped by the tide,
Still wave-damp: like an eye
Reflecting the pale,
The furry images
    Of the northern sky.

2

There on the empty golden lawns
Soon to be confetti-thick with people,
He would ride one beast
While the others followed
In a world fit for donkeys.
There he jolted and rolled and bumped and trotted,
And threw stones for the dogs, so that they ran into the water,
Frightening the peering, pecking, tearing sea-gulls
Clad in their feathers of sea and sky.

Later, they waited impatiently, he and his drove,
Until a party chartered them,
Then at last he would run beside the donkeys, on the level,
Cursing them though he loved them,
Shouting,
    Warding them off the wrong direction
                With a stout stick,
Amid the jostled cries and laughter.   *Osbert Sitwell*

The Bubble

I blew myself a bubble
    That was bigger than myself
And I floated up inside it
    To the top-most shelf,

And there I saw before me
    With my own two eyes
Half a hundred jam-pots
    And four dead flies.

I blew myself a bubble
    That was larger than Papa
And he floated off inside it
    To a place afar,

As everybody cheered and waved
    To see him overhead
'Your Father is a very clever man,'
    They said.
                  Kenneth Hopkins

A Memory

When I was as high as that
I saw a poet in his hat.
I think the poet must have smiled
At such a solemn gazing child.

Now wasn't it a funny thing
To get a sight of J. M. Synge,
And notice nothing but his hat?
Yet life is often queer like that.
                  L. A. G. Strong

J. M. Synge (1871–1909) was the Irish playwright who wrote *The Playboy of the Western World*. L. A. G. Strong reminds us very tactfully how to pronounce his name.

Farm Child

Look at this village boy, his head is stuffed
With all the nests he knows, his pockets with flowers.
Snail-shells and bits of glass, the fruit of hours
Spent in the fields by thorn and thistle tuft.
Look at his eyes, see the harebell hiding there;
Mark how the sun has freckled his smooth face
Like a finch's egg under that bush of hair
That dares the wind, and in the mixen now
Notice his poise; from such unconscious grace
Earth breeds and beckons to the stubborn plough.

R. S. Thomas

Cynddylan on a Tractor

Ah, you should see Cynddylan on a tractor.
Gone the old look that yoked him to the soil;
He's a new man now, part of the machine,
His nerves of metal and his blood oil.
The clutch curses, but the gears obey
His least bidding, and lo, he's away
Out of the farmyard, scattering hens.
Riding to work now as a great man should,
He is the knight at arms breaking the fields'
Mirror of silence, emptying the wood
Of foxes and squirrels and bright jays.
The sun comes over the tall trees
Kindling all the hedges, but not for him
Who runs his engine on a different fuel.
And all the birds are singing, bills wide in vain,
As Cynddylan passes proudly up the lane.

R. S. Thomas

Cynddylan is pronounced Cun-thullan.

78

A Parting Shot

He said, 'Do not point your gun
At the dove in the judas tree :
It might go off, you see.'

So I fired, and the tree came down –
Limed leaf, branch and stock,
And the fantail swerving flew
Up like a shuttlecock
Released into the blue.

And he said, 'I told you so.'

C. Day Lewis

My parents kept me from children who were rough

My parents kept me from children who were rough
Who threw words like stones and who wore torn clothes.
Their thighs showed through rags. They ran in the street
And climbed cliffs and stripped by the country streams.

I feared more than tigers their muscles like iron
Their jerking hands and their knees tight on my arms.
I feared the salt coarse pointing of those boys
Who copied my lisp behind me on the road.

They were lithe, they sprang out behind hedges
Like dogs to bark at my world. They threw mud
While I looked the other way, pretending to smile.
I longed to forgive them, but they never smiled.

Stephen Spender

The Collier

When I was born on Amman hill
A dark bird crossed the sun.
Sharp on the floor the shadow fell;
I was the youngest son.

And when I went to the County School
I worked in a shaft of light.
In the wood of the desk I cut my name :
Dai for Dynamite.

The tall black hills my brothers stood;
Their lessons all were done.
From the door of the school when I ran out
They frowned to watch me run.

The slow grey bells they rung a chime
Surly with grief or age.
Clever or clumsy, lad or lout,
All would look for a wage.

I learnt the valley flowers' names
And the rough bark knew my knees.
I brought home trout from the river
And spotted eggs from the trees.

A coloured coat I was given to wear
Where the lights of the rough land shone.
Still jealous of my favour
The tall black hills looked on.

They dipped my coat in the blood of a kid
And they cast me down a pit,
And although I crossed with strangers
There was no way up from it.

Soon as I went from the County School
I worked in a shaft. Said Jim,
'You will get your chain of gold, my lad,
But not for a likely time.'

And one said, 'Jack was not raised up
When the wind blew out the light
Though he interpreted their dreams
And guessed their fears by night.'

And Tom, he shivered his leper's lamp
For the stain that round him grew;
And I heard mouths pray in the after-damp
When the picks would not break through.

They changed words there in darkness
And still through my head they run,
And white on my limbs is the linen sheet
And gold on my neck the sun.

Vernon Watkins

Clowns

Clowns, Clowns and
Clowns
A firm that furthers
Nobody's business

Zanies by royal
Charter and adept
At false addition
And gay combustion

With bladders for batons
And upright eyebrows
Flappers for feet
And figs for no one.

The child's face pops
Like ginger beer
To see the air
Alive with bowlers.

Bric-a-brac
Pick-a-back
Spillbucket
Splits.

Louis MacNeice

Hunter Trials

It's awf'lly bad luck on Diana,
    Her ponies have swallowed their bits;
She fished down their throats with a spanner
    And frightened them all into fits.

So now she's attempting to borrow.
   Do lend her some bits, Mummy, *do*;
I'll lend her my own for to-morrow,
   But to-day *I*'ll be wanting them too.

Just look at Prunella on Guzzle,
   The wizardest pony on earth;
Why doesn't she slacken his muzzle
   And tighten the breech in his girth?

I say, Mummy, there's Mrs Geyser
   And doesn't she look pretty sick?
I bet it's because Mona Lisa
   Was hit on the hock with a brick.

Miss Blewitt says Monica threw it,
   But Monica says it was Joan,
And Joan's very thick with Miss Blewitt,
   So Monica's sulking alone.

And Margaret failed in her paces,
   Her withers got tied in a noose,
So her coronets caught in the traces
   And now all her fetlocks are loose.

Oh, it's me now. I'm terribly nervous.
   I wonder if Smudges will shy.
She's practically certain to swerve as
   Her Pelham is over one eye.

*   *   *   *

Oh wasn't it naughty of Smudges?
   Oh, Mummy, I'm sick with disgust.
She threw me in front of the Judges,
   And my silly old collarbone's bust.

John Betjeman

Harrow-on-the-Hill

When melancholy Autumn comes to Wembley
   And electric trains are lighted after tea
The poplars near the Stadium are trembly
    With their tap and tap and whispering to me,
      Like the sound of little breakers
      Spreading out along the surf-line
When the estuary's filling
    With the sea.

Then Harrow-on-the-Hill's a rocky island
   And Harrow churchyard full of sailors' graves
And the constant click and kissing of the trolley buses hissing
   Is the level to the Wealdstone turned to waves
      And the rumble of the railway
      Is the thunder of the rollers
As they gather up for plunging
    Into caves.

There's a storm cloud to the westward over Kenton,
   There's a line of harbour lights at Perivale,
Is it rounding rough Pentire in a flood of sunset fire
   The little fleet of trawlers under sail?
      Can those boats be only roof tops
      As they stream along the skyline
In a race for port and Padstow
    With the gale?

John Betjeman

The seaside in this poem is on the estuary of the River Camel, on the North Coast of Cornwall, where John Betjeman spent a good deal of his childhood. He still returns there whenever he can.

Autobiographical Fragment

When I lived down in Devonshire
    The callers at my cottage
Were Constant Angst, the art critic,
    And old Major Courage.

Angst always brought me something nice
    To get in my good graces :
A quilt, a roll of cotton-wool,
    A pair of dark glasses.

He tore up all my unpaid bills,
    Went and got my slippers,
Took the telephone off its hook
    And bolted up the shutters.

We smoked and chatted by the fire,
    Sometimes just nodding;
His charming presence made it right
    To sit and do nothing.

But then – those awful afternoons
    I walked out with the Major !
I ran up hills, down streams, through briars;
    It was sheer blue murder.

Trim in his boots, riding-breeches
    And threadbare Norfolk jacket,
He watched me, frowning, bawled commands
    To work hard and enjoy it.

I asked him once why I was there,
    Except to get all dirty;
He tugged his grey moustache and snapped :
    'Young man, it's your duty.'

What duty's served by pointless, mad
    Climbing and crawling?
I tell you, I was thankful when
    The old bore stopped calling.

Kingsley Amis

Confusions of the Alphabet

Capital I gave a party
capital U came along
capital O stepped in between
and threw the reckoning wrong.

Capital G went walking
with capitals O and D
dodging the traffic, they got reversed
spelt out the contrary.

Capital I gave a party
but this time nobody came
capital I sat down and tried
to think up a solo game:

I didn't fancy living
with no one to sit beside
so I lay down and died.

John Wain

Emperors of the Island

There is the story of a deserted island
where five men walked down to the bay.

The story of this island is
that three men would two men slay.

Three men dug two graves in the sand,
three men stood on the sea wet rock,
three shadows moved away.

There is the story of a deserted island
where three men walked down to the bay.

The story of this island is
that two men would one man slay.

Two men dug one grave in the sand,
two men stood on the sea wet rock,
two shadows moved away.

There is the story of a deserted island
where two men walked down to the bay.

The story of this island is
that one man would one man slay.

One man dug one grave in the sand,
one man stood on the sea wet rock,
one shadow moved away.

There is the story of a deserted island
where four ghosts walked down to the bay.

The story of this island is
that four ghosts would one man slay.

Four ghosts dug one grave in the sand,
four ghosts stood on the sea wet rock;
five ghosts moved away.   *Dannie Abse*

Emperors of the Island is a poem written to be read aloud: so
please try it this way. Dannie Abse calls it 'a political parable'.

Horses on the Camargue

To A. F. Tschiffely

In the grey wastes of dread,
The haunt of shattered gulls where nothing moves
But in a shroud of silence like the dead,
I heard a sudden harmony of hooves,
And, turning, saw afar
A hundred snowy horses unconfined,
The silver runaways of Neptune's car
Racing, spray-curled, like waves before the wind.
Sons of the Mistral, fleet
As him with whose strong gusts they love to flee,
Who shod the flying thunders on their feet
And plumed them with the snortings of the sea;
Theirs is no earthly breed
Who only haunt the verges of the earth
And only on the sea's salt herbage feed –
Surely the great white breakers gave them birth.
For when for years a slave,
A horse of the Camargue, in alien lands,
Should catch some far-off fragrance of the wave
Carried far inland from his native sands,
Many have told the tale
Of how in fury, foaming at the rein,
He hurls his rider; and with lifted tail,
With coal-red eyes and cataracting mane,
Heading his course for home,
Though sixty foreign leagues before him sweep,
Will never rest until he breathes the foam
And hears the native thunder of the deep.
But when the great gusts rise
And lash their anger on these arid coasts,
When the scared gulls career with mournful cries
And whirl across the waste like driven ghosts :

When hail and fire converge,
The only souls to which they strike no pain
Are the white-crested fillies of the surge
And the white horses of the windy plain.
Then in their strength and pride
The stallions of the wilderness rejoice;
They feel their Master's trident in their side,
And high and shrill they answer to his voice.
With white tails smoking free,
Long streaming manes, and arching necks, they show
Their kinship to their sisters of the sea –
And forward hurl their thunderbolts of snow.
Still out of hardship bred,
Spirits of power and beauty and delight
Have ever on such frugal pastures fed
And loved to course with tempests through the night.

Roy Campbell

The Camargue is an area of just under 300 square miles at the mouth of the Rhône in the south of France. Part of it is swamp-land, part is used for growing wine and grain, and the rest is used as a huge grazing ground for thousands of horses and cattle, including wild bulls. The cowboys are called *gardiens*, wear check-shirts, cart-wheel hats, and control the cattle with long tridents or metal-pointed staves. When Roy Campbell writes of the cream-coloured horses as they 'feel their Master's trident in their side' he is thinking not only of the *gardien's* trident but also the trident of Neptune, King of the Sea. He sees the wild horses as 'the silver runaways of Neptune's car', or chariot. When, again, he calls them 'Sons of the Mistral' he is speaking of the cold Mistral wind that blows down the valley of the River Rhône, with the Camarguais horses galloping as fast as the wind itself.

Les Saintes-Maries-de-la-Mer

The boats as Van Gogh painted them,
Slashed scarlet, cobalt, cinnamon, bows
Facing the Camargue, the sea at their backs.
Only along the looped breakers
Gipsies in lines, like the lost tribes,
Sit eating over wood fires.

To-day they followed in procession,
Coming to the water for blessing, bearing
Images of saints on their shoulders,
And the *gardiens* in checked shirts
Rode off the crowd, believing
And not believing, photographing the gipsies
Whose pilgrimage it was.

Fires in the encampment, hoarse flamenco
At night. Candlesticks, nougat,
Rifle-ranges by day. And the thin sea
Breaking salt on the marshes, secretive
With ibis and crane and flamingo.

Religion and games of skill as distractions,
Confident trappings and a hangdog faith
In getting something out of it,
But always in the end falling back
On the picturesque elements, the *jeu*
De bouquets on white ponies, women
In neckerchiefs and stiff brocade blouses,
Admiring ritual for ritual's sake;
                    Tarot and roulette,
A flurry of swings and loud music,
The roundabouts bright as Van Gogh's boats,
Enjoyment selling itself on whoever's behalf.

At night rain damps out the fires.
And the gipsies, believing and
Not believing, move on till next year.
Only the church, floodlit, sails like a galleon through darkness.

Alan Ross

The two Saint Maries were the sister of the Blessed Virgin Mary, and the mother of James and John. They are said to have come with their black servant Sarah and settled near the mouth of the River Rhône after the crucifixion of Jesus. Here, it is believed, they also built a church.

Today, Les Saintes-Maries-de-la-Mer is a seaside town. The Dutch painter Vincent van Gogh (1853–1890) made some of his most famous drawings and paintings of the fishing-boats on the beach here. In the crypt of the church there stands a black figure of Sarah. Her memory is very much venerated by the gipsies, who come here in thousands from all parts of Europe once a year to pay tribute to their patron saint. They hold a service in the crypt, and no non-gipsy is allowed to enter. A great fair is also held. There is *flamenco* singing and dancing, games such as roulette or the *jeu de bouquets*, and fortune-telling. For the fortune-telling a special kind of card, the tarot playing-card, is used. Nearby, on the Camargue, is a great lagoon that is also a famous nature reserve for wild-birds.

Kurdish Shepherds

They squat silhouetted against the hills,
A handful of men with rifles, sharp-nosed
And dark, with pale blue turbans whose frills
Hang down on their shoulders, as if they were posed.

They might have been there for ever, lost
In their spiritual mnemonics, herds grazing
At will or wandering beneath them on mossed
And irregular plains – till sunset drops in a flare
Illumining them, suddenly making their world amazing.

Alan Ross

Santa Maria Maggiore, Rome

According to the legend, snow fell on the Esquiline Hill in August A.D. 358 as a sign that a great Basilica was to be built there

Say the snow drifted down
On the Esquiline Hill in August and the light
    Easily changed to winter. Say the hill
    Heaved for a moment over the town
And suddenly in the dear defeated night
      The snow was still.

    So I could well believe
Watching it now, the church completed there,
    Altered and added to but still the same;
    Senses and not the heart deceive –
Snow grown solid and grey in the Easter air.
      I think there came

    Once to the Pope and king
Who set the great basilica upright
A snowstorm in their hot and summer sleep
    That when they woke they swore to bring
Such solid coolness to that sultry light
      As snowdrifts deep.

Elizabeth Jennings

A basilica is a church of a special shape. This is usually an oblong hall, with double rows of columns, and an apse at one end. An apse is a recess with a domed or a vaulted roof.

5 Occasions, Seasons and Festivals

ARIES (Mar. 21 to April 19).—
on't expect spectacular result
n work you have just com
d. But rewards are on th

CANCER (June 21-July 21).—It
be hard to make much impression
other people, either in business
socially

time to try to revive the past in
way; but a good day for making
contacts.

LEO (July 22-August 21).—Not
your programme as possible.

April 20 to May 20
you now to sho
e still capable
heir wishes.

21 to June 21
ard against ca
Make every penn

22 to July 21
lf measures, b
asis in th
rmation is

Sept. 22
very respe
king in t
nd th
a b

(Aug. 21):
eriors:
early: yo
ll be e
ar all

to Oct. 22
you meet at
may solve a pre
or you

Nov. 21
and upc
for yo
which yo

(Nov. 22 to De
at work: this con
the wrong impre

(Dec. 22 to Ja
too forceful

(Jan. 21 to Fe
you have no se
years will bring gre

PISCES (Feb. 20 to Mar. 20
Don't rush matters An answ
to the particular question cou
be forthcoming in a day or tw
Delay decisions until then.

IF YOUR CHILD WAS BOR
MAY 8

Early Astir

Early, early I walked in the city :
The river ran its strength from misty valleys
And the sun lit the wings of stone angels.

Yarrol! Yarrol! I cried exultingly :
Passing dogs lifted wet noses
And housemaidens the blinds of their gables.

Herbert Read

April Fool

As the April fool came over the hill
The weather spoke aloud :
It placed a sunny weathercock
Against a livid cloud.

Then the rain swam down like pilot-fish,
The lightning bit like sharks,
The grass rushed out of doors to see
All over the green parks . . .

The cloud had sunk from memory,
The blue sail filled with a breeze;
He saw the errands of all birds,
The husbandry of bees.

The ploughland lay refined dust,
The sower flung the grains,
The birds came tumbling out of air
And took their pirate gains.

The pigeon clapped his hands, the gull
Turned living in the sun.
The blackthorn was a thousand pounds.
The April fool looked on.

As the April fool went under the hill
The weather spoke aloud,
It backed an inky weathercock
On a white cotton cloud.

Hal Summers

Pilot-fish are the little fish that dart along in front of a shark.

Hearing the Cuckoo

For Frank and Rosalind Heywood

Cuckoo, bubbling your green words across half Berkshire
And the gardens decorated with Japanese cherry,
You hobo-bird, who hitch your sparehawk wings
To the gilded horns of the April sun – O drunken cuckoo,
Suck the sweet flowers, keep your voice clear, to spill
Your double-talk over the landscapes, idle
As any poet on a Holy Saturday!

John Heath-Stubbs

'Sparehawk' is a dialect variant of 'sparrow-hawk'.

April Day: Binsey

Now the year's let loose; it skips like a feckless child,
Ruffles our hair, rouses the trees, runs wild,
Kisses the hills with sunlight, whips them with rain,
Teases the grass in passing, gets lost in the lane.
Taut as lyre-strings the swans' wings quiver,
Lyre-strings plucked by the wind on the swollen river.
Shadows of clouds and cantering horses race
Over the meadows where heaven and earth embrace.

Michael Hamburger

Michael Hamburger wrote this poem during a visit to Oxford
and a walk to Binsey, which is famous for its poplars.

Herding Lambs

(To O.)

In the spring, in the morning,
We heard the high bleat,
And the low voice of the ewes, and the rainlike
Rustle of feet.

In the daffodil day
My sister called to me,
And out to the garden gate
We went to see.

No dogs, no sticks,
No shouting, no noise,
Only the rustle, the bleating,
The chirping boys.

Slowly they moved along,
Herded by three
Old grey men, and five children,
To the fresh lea.

And when a silly lamb
Turned back in fright
A withered or an infant hand
Guided him right.

The early mist muffled their sound,
Muted that double chime
Trembling along the grassy ground
From the morning of time.

Ruth Pitter

May Day

Winter rose, and in one night fled away.
The buds rushed into leaf on every spray.
Green was a new colour, you would say.
The air was filled with gold-dust and careless music.
Certainly it was some sort of festal day.

The spirit of maytime was a girl in blue.
'In whose honour,' I asked, 'is all this to-do?'
'In yours,' she answered, 'in yours' – and her smile died.
'Did you not know?' she sobbed. 'It is all for you.'

James Reeves

The Old Ones

In the May evening
Flowing with golden light,
Out went the old woman
To meditate;

Pottered through the orchard,
Her cat at her side –
So old the two of them,
Time they died.

But when they sat them down on the bench
Under an apple-tree,
'Here we are,' said the old woman,
'Where we belong to be.'

Blossom floated from the branches,
Light as snowflakes touched those two friends.
Coarsened fur and faded hair
And bent transparent hands.

So they sat, the two of them,
In some content . . .
The violent bats swerved to and fro,
The brightness went,

Leaving the sky as any shell
Delicate and pure;
Soundless flitted past the moths
Through the dim blossomy air.

Yet still, still, those old ones –
As if the sun still shone –
Sat there, never noticing
Another day had gone.

'Here we are,' said the old woman,
'Under the apple-tree
'On this sweet May evening,
'Where we belong to be.'

Frances Bellerby

The words 'Where we belong to be' in this poem are used in the
Cornish way. Frances Bellerby says this includes, 'Where we are
accustomed to be, where we are at home, where we *ought* to
be : having a perfect right to be there' – a perfectly accurate
description. The old woman lived with her cat in the same
Cornish village as Frances Bellerby at that time. As an example
of the way in which poems come to be written, it is interesting
that the poet says of this one, 'In no way was the poem made
because of them. It might be nearer truth to say that they were
found in the poem when it came to be written.'

The old cat died about a year later, aged 17, and was buried
under the apple-tree.

The Haystack

Too dense to have a door,
Window or fireplace or a floor,
They saw this cottage up,
Huge bricks of grass, clover and buttercup
Carting to byre and stable,
Where cow and horse will eat wall, roof and gable.

Andrew Young

If you came

If you came to my secret glade,
    Weary with heat,
I would set you down in the shade,
    I would wash your feet.

If you came in the winter sad,
    Wanting for bread,
I would give you the last that I had,
    I would give you my bed.

But the place is hidden apart
    Like a nest by a brook,
And I will not show you my heart
    By a word, by a look.

The place is hidden apart
    Like the nest of a bird:
And I will not show you my heart
    By a look, by a word.

Ruth Pitter

The Hut

Whatever place is poor and small,
The Hut was poorer still,
Stuck, like a snail upon a wall,
On what we called a hill.

It leaned upon an apple-tree
Whose laden branches lay
On the hot roof voluptuously,
And murmured all the day.

One hand-broad window, full of boughs,
Mirrored the flaming hearth
As if the Dryad warmed her house
With fire from under earth;

And one the livid lasting-pea
And staring marigold,
The knotty oak and elder-tree
Showed in the morning cold.

The sapling ash had mined the floor,
The chimney flew the bine;
The doorway was without a door,
But flaunted eglantine.

The swallow built upon the beam,
The rat was much at home:
And there one foolish child would dream,
Where sorrow could not come.

Ruth Pitter

Ruth Pitter says about *The Hut*, 'If you look at the stanza which
begins "One hand-broad window, full of boughs," remember you
are looking through the tiny window at the tree outside, and at
the same time seeing the reflection of the fire in it, as though
the Dryad (the spirit of the tree) actually had a home with a fire
burning, up there among the leaves.'

Poem in October

It was my thirtieth year to heaven
Woke to my hearing from harbour and neighbour wood
And the mussel pooled and the heron
Priested shore
The morning beckon
With water praying and call of seagull and rook
And the knock of sailing boats on the net webbed wall
Myself to set foot
That second
In the still sleeping town and set forth.

My birthday began with the water-
Birds and the birds of the winged trees flying my name
Above the farms and the white horses
And I rose
In rainy autumn
And walked abroad in a shower of all my days.
High tide and the heron dived when I took the road
Over the border
And the gates
Of the town closed as the town awoke.

A springful of larks in a rolling
Cloud and the roadside bushes brimming with whistling
Blackbirds and the sun of October
Summery
On the hill's shoulder,
Here were fond climates and sweet singers suddenly
Come in the morning where I wandered and listened
To the rain wringing
Wind blow cold
In the wood faraway under me.

102

Pale rain over the dwindling harbour
And over the sea wet church the size of a snail
With its horns through mist and the castle
Brown as owls
But all the gardens
Of spring and summer were blooming in the tall tales
Beyond the border and under the lark full cloud.
There could I marvel
My birthday
Away but the weather turned around.

It turned away from the blithe country
And down the other air and the blue altered sky
Streamed again a wonder of summer
With apples
Pears and red currants
And I saw in the turning so clearly a child's
Forgotten mornings when he walked with his mother
Through the parables
Of sun light
And the legends of the green chapels

And the twice told fields of infancy
That his tears burned my cheeks and his heart moved in mine.
These were the woods the river and sea
Where a boy
In the listening
Summertime of the dead whispered the truth of his joy
To the trees and the stones and the fish in the tide.
And the mystery
Sang alive
Still in the water and singingbirds.

And there could I marvel my birthday
Away but the weather turned around. And the true

Joy of the long dead child sang burning
In the sun.
It was my thirtieth
Year to heaven stood there then in the summer noon
Though the town below lay leaved with October blood.
O may my heart's truth
Still be sung
On this high hill in a year's turning.

Dylan Thomas

Fifth of November

The children celebrate a failure and a treason,
And make the grown-ups turn it into
Bangs and coloured lights in the dark drizzle,
A party and a holiday.

For the grown-ups have nothing to celebrate,
Nothing to transform
Into the bonfire's circle, the charm against the dark:

If they drew near, their failure might dowse the fire,
And their treason
Still crouches in a cellar, waiting to be caught.

K. W. Gransden

Weather Ear

Lying in bed in the dark, I hear the bray
Of the furnace hooter rasping the slates, and say :
'The wind will be in the east, and frost on the nose, today.'

Or when, in the still, small, conscience hours, I hear
The market clock-bell clacking close to my ear :
'A north-west wind from the fell, and the sky-light swilled and clear.

But now when the roofs are sulky as the dead,
With a snuffle and sniff in the gullies, a drip on the lead :
'No wind at all, and the street stone-deaf with a cold in the head.'

Norman Nicholson

Prelude

The winter evening settles down
With smell of steaks in passageways.
Six o'clock.
The burnt-out ends of smoky days.
And now a gusty shower wraps
The grimy scraps
Of withered leaves about your feet
And newspapers from vacant lots;
The showers beat
On broken blinds and chimney-pots,
And at the corner of the street
A lonely cab-horse steams and stamps.
And then the lighting of the lamps.

T. S. Eliot

In Memory of Jane Fraser

When snow like sheep lay in the fold
And winds went begging at each door,
And the far hills were blue with cold,
And a cold shroud lay on the moor,

She kept the siege. And every day
We watched her brooding over death
Like a strong bird above its prey.
The room filled with the kettle's breath.

Damp curtains glued against the pane
Sealed time away. Her body froze
As if to freeze us all, and chain
Creation to a stunned repose.

She died before the world could stir.
In March the ice unloosed the brook
And water ruffled the sun's hair,
And a few sprinkled leaves unshook.

Geoffrey Hill

When asked if Jane Fraser was a real person, Geoffrey Hill replied: 'Jane Fraser is no-one in particular: she is an amalgam of childhood memories of farm-kitchens, poker-backed aunts, etc., and the finest thing Charlotte Brontë ever wrote – her valediction to Emily.'

A valediction is a saying of farewell. Emily Brontë died aged thirty at Haworth Parsonage, Yorkshire, in 1848, the year after her one novel, *Wuthering Heights*, was published. Charlotte Brontë wrote *Jane Eyre*. Her valediction to Emily reads: 'Never in all her life had she lingered over any task that lay before her, and she did not linger now. She sank rapidly. She made haste to leave us. Yet, while physically she perished, mentally she grew stronger than we had yet known her. Day by day, when I saw with what a front she met suffering, I looked on her with an anguish of wonder and love. I have seen nothing like it; but, indeed, I have never seen her parallel in anything. Stronger than a man, simpler than a child, her nature stood alone.'

The Eve of Christmas

It was the evening before the night
That Jesus turned from dark to light.

Joseph was walking round and round,
And yet he moved not on the ground.

He looked into the heavens, and saw
The pole stood silent, star on star.

He looked into the forest: there
The leaves hung dead upon the air.

He looked into the sea, and found
It frozen, and the lively fishes bound.

And in the sky, the birds that sang
Not in feathered clouds did hang.

Said Joseph: 'What is this silence all?'
An angel spoke: 'It is no thrall,

But is a sign of great delight:
The Prince of Love is born this night.'

And Joseph said: 'Where may I find
This wonder?' – 'He is all mankind,

Look, he is both farthest, nearest,
Highest and lowest, of all men the dearest.'

Then Joseph moved, and found the stars
Moved with him, and the evergreen airs,

The birds went flying, and the main
Flowed with its fishes once again.

And everywhere they went, they cried:
'Love lives, when all had died!'

In Excelsis Gloria!

James Kirkup

Christmas Day

Last night in the open shippen
    The Infant Jesus lay,
While cows stood at the hay-crib
    Twitching the sweet hay.

As I trudged through the snow-fields
    That lay in their own light,
A thorn-bush with its shadow
    Stood doubled on the night.

And I stayed on my journey
    To listen to the cheep
Of a small bird in the thorn-bush
    I woke from its puffed sleep.

The bright stars were my angels
    And with the heavenly host
I sang praise to the Father,
    The Son and Holy Ghost.

Andrew Young

African Christmas

Here are no signs of festival,
No holly and no mistletoe,
No robin and no crackling fire,
And no soft, feathery fall of snow.

In England one could read the words
Telling how shepherds in the fold
Followed the star and reached the barn
Which kept the Saviour from the cold,

And picture in one's mind the scene –
The tipsy, cheerful foreign troops,
The kindly villagers who stood
About the Child in awkward groups.

But in this blazing Christmas heat
The ox, the ass, the bed of hay
The shepherds and the Holy Child
Are stilted figures in a play.

Exiles, we see that we, like slaves
To symbol and to memory,
Have worshipped, not the incarnate Christ,
But tinsel on the Christmas tree.

John Press

At Christmas, 1943, John Press was stationed with the Royal
Artillery at Mombasa in the tropical region of East Africa,
he says, December is about the hottest month of all.

Innocent's Song

Who's that knocking on the window,
Who's that standing at the door,
What are all those presents
Lying on the kitchen floor?

Who is the smiling stranger
With hair as white as gin,
What is he doing with the children
And who could have let him in?

Why has he rubies on his fingers,
A cold, cold crown on his head,
Why, when he caws his carol,
Does the salty snow run red?

Why does he ferry my fireside
As a spider on a thread,
His fingers made of fuses
And his tongue of gingerbread?

Why does the world before him
Melt in a million suns,
Why do his yellow, yearning eyes
Burn like saffron buns?

Watch where he comes walking
Out of the Christmas flame,
Dancing, double-talking:

Herod is his name.

Charles Causley

In *Innocent's Song* the central character keeps changing into
someone or something else. The mysterious stranger becomes
the jolly and kind Father Christmas, who in turn becomes King
Herod. On 28th December we remember the Holy Innocents,
murdered by Herod when he was searching for the Infant Jesus.
Then the King becomes the symbol of the destroying bomb.

My joy, my jockey, my Gabriel

My joy, my jockey, my Gabriel
Who bares his horns above my sleep
Is sleeping now. And I shall keep him
In valley and on pinnacle
And marvellous in my tabernacle.

My peace is where his shoulder holds
My clouds among his skies of face;
His plenty is my peace, my peace :
And like a serpent by a boulder
His shade I rest in glory coiled.

Time will divide us, and the sea
Wring its wild hands all day between;
The autumn bring a change of scene.
But always and for ever he
At night will sleep and keep by me.

George Barker

THE CONTRIBUTORS

DANNIE ABSE was born in Cardiff, South Wales, in 1923. He has published novels and plays as well as poetry, and recent collections of his verse are *A Small Desperation* (1968) and *Selected Poems* (1970). As well as being a writer, Dannie Abse is also a doctor and he lives and works in London.

KINGSLEY AMIS was born in London in 1922, and educated at City of London School and St John's College, Oxford. He served in the Army, 1942–5, was Lecturer in English, University College of Swansea and Fellow in English at Peterhouse, Cambridge. He has also taught in the U.S.A. His books of poems include *A Case of Samples* (1956) and *A Look Round the Estate* (1967); and his many novels include *Lucky Jim* (1954).

W. H. AUDEN was born in 1907, educated at Gresham's School, Holt, and Christ Church, Oxford. In recent years he has divided his time between New York, Italy, and Austria. He was Professor of Poetry at the University of Oxford 1956–61, and he has been the recipient of very many literary honours and awards. His *Collected Shorter Poems, 1927–1957* appeared in 1966; and recent years have also seen the appearance of his *Collected Longer Poems* (1968), *Selected Poems* (1968), and *City Without Walls* (1969). In collaboration with Christopher Isherwood, he wrote the verse-plays *The Dog Beneath the Skin* (1935), *The Ascent of F.6* (1936), *On the Frontier* (1938); and with Chester Kallman, the libretti of the operas *The Rake's Progress*, music by Igor Stravinsky (1951), and *The Magic Flute* by Mozart (1956).

GEORGE BARKER was born in Loughton, Essex, in 1913, and educated at Marlborough Road London County Council School, Chelsea, and at the Regent Street Polytechnic, London. He was Professor of English Literature at Imperial Tohoku University, Japan (1939–41), and was Visiting Professor at New York State University, 1965–6. His books of verse include *Dreams of a Summer Night* (1966) and *The Golden Chains* (1968). He has also published two collections of verse for children: *Runes and Rhymes and Tunes and Chimes* (1969), and *To Aylsham Fair* (1970).

FRANCES BELLERBY was born in 1899 in Bristol, spent many years in Cornwall, and now lives near Kingsbridge in South Devon. She is also a novelist, and has published three collections of short stories. Her books of verse include *The Stone Angel and the Stone Man* (1958) and *Selected Poems* (1971).

SIR JOHN BETJEMAN was born in London in 1906 and was educated at Marlborough and at Oxford. He lives at Wantage, in Berkshire. His autobiography in verse, *Summoned by Bells*, was published in 1960, and the most recent edition of his Collected Poems appeared in 1970. In addition to his poetry, he has written and edited many books on the British countryside and on architecture, and is an Honorary Associate of the Royal Institute of British Architects. He has received a number of literary awards, including the Queen's Gold Medal for Poetry in 1960, and he was made a Companion of Literature, Royal Society of Literature, in 1968. He was knighted in 1969.

THOMAS BLACKBURN was born in 1916 at Hensingham in Cumberland, where his father was vicar. He was educated at Bromsgrove School and at Durham University. After some years as a schoolteacher, he is now Principal Lecturer in English at the College of St Mark and St John, London. His most recent collections of verse are *A Smell of Burning* (1961), *A Breathing Space* (1964) and *The Fourth Man* (1971). He has also published books of literary criticism and edited a number of anthologies of modern poetry, and in 1969 published an autobiographical novel, *A Clip of Steel*.

ROY CAMPBELL was born in Durban, Natal, in 1901, and educated at Durban High School, and at Natal University. He first came to Europe in 1919, and lived much of his life in France, Spain, and Portugal. He fought in the Spanish Civil War, and in the Second World War was with the Royal Welch Fusiliers and the South Wales Borderers, and served in East and North Africa. His autobiography, *Light on a Dark Horse*, was published in 1951, and volumes of his *Collected Poems* in 1949, 1957, and 1960. He was killed in a motoring accident in Portugal in 1957.

CHARLES CAUSLEY was born in 1917 at Launceston, Cornwall, where he still writes and teaches. He served in the Royal Navy, 1940–6. He is a Fellow of the Royal Society of Literature, and in

1967 was awarded the Queen's Gold Medal for Poetry. Recent collections of his verse are *Underneath the Water* (1968), *Figure of 8* (narrative poems, 1969), and *Figgie Hobbin* (1971). He has also edited a number of anthologies of modern verse, including a companion volume to *Dawn and Dusk*: a collection of story poems and ballads of the twentieth century, *Rising Early* (1964).

LEONARD CLARK was born in 1905 at St Peter Port, Guernsey, brought up in Gloucestershire, and educated at Monmouth School, and Normal College, Bangor. At present he lives in London, and was for many years an H.M. Inspector of Schools. His numerous books include studies of the poets Walter de la Mare and Andrew Young, and three volumes of autobiography, *Green Wood* (1962), *A Fool in the Forest* (1965), and *Grateful Caliban* (1968). His *Selected Poems 1940–1957* appeared in 1958, and he has also written many books of verse for children and edited a large number of verse anthologies. He is a Fellow of the Royal Society of Literature, and is a Freeman of the City of London.

T. S. ELIOT, O.M., was born in 1888 at St Louis, U.S.A., and educated at Harvard University, the Sorbonne, and Merton College, Oxford. The recipient of many academic awards and distinctions, he received the Nobel Prize for Literature in 1948. His plays include *Murder in the Cathedral* (1935), *The Cocktail Party* (1950), *The Confidential Clerk* (1954), and *The Elder Statesman* (1959). He published many volumes of essays and criticism; his *Four Quartets* appeared in 1944 and his *Collected Poems 1909–62* in 1963. His verse also includes *Old Possum's Book of Practical Cats* (1939). T. S. Eliot died in 1965.

ROY FULLER was born at Failsworth in 1912, and was educated at private schools. He served in the Royal Navy, 1941–6, and worked as a solicitor in London until 1969. His *Collected Poems* appeared in 1962, and subsequent books of verse are *Buff* (1965) and *New Poems* (1968). He has also written a number of novels, including three for children. In 1968 he was elected Professor of Poetry at Oxford University, and in 1970 he received the Queen's Gold Medal for Poetry.

K. W. GRANSDEN was born in 1925 at Herne Bay, Kent. He began writing verse at the age of eighteen while serving in the

Army during the Second World War, and continued at Cambridge. He has been a teacher, Assistant Keeper of Manuscripts at the British Museum, and Literary Editor of *The Listener*. He is at present a member of the English Department at Warwick University. A collection of his verse, *Any Day*, appeared in 1960, and his books of literary criticism include studies of John Donne, E. M. Forster, and Tennyson's *In Memoriam*.

ROBERT GRAVES was born at Wimbledon in 1895 and educated at Charterhouse and St John's College, Oxford. He served during the First World War with the Royal Welch Fusiliers (on one occasion he was officially reported dead), and now lives in Majorca, Spain. He published his autobiography *Goodbye to All That* in 1929, and in a revised version in 1957. He has written many historical novels, including *I, Claudius* (1934), *Sergeant Lamb of The Ninth* (1940), and *King Jesus* (1946). He was awarded the Hawthornden and James Tait Black Memorial Prizes for *Claudius the God* (1934) and *Count Belisarius* (1938), and has received many other honours and distinctions, including the Queen's Gold Medal for Poetry in 1968. He was Professor of Poetry at Oxford, 1961–6. His essays and opinions on poetry are to be found in *The White Goddess* (1947), *The Common Asphodel* (1949), and *The Crowning Privilege* (1955). Recent volumes of his verse are *Collected Poems 1965* (1965), *Love Respelt* (1965), *Poems 1965–1968* (1968), and *Poems 1968–70* (1970).

MICHAEL HAMBURGER was born in Berlin in 1924, educated there and in Edinburgh and London, and at Christ Church, Oxford. He served in the Army, 1943–7. He is married, with three children, and was for some time Reader in German at Reading University. He is also a translator and critic, and has published a good deal of work in this capacity. Recent collections of his verse include *Weather and Season* (1963) and *Travelling* (1969).

JOHN HEATH-STUBBS was born in London in 1918, but lived at New Milton, Hampshire, from the age of six to that of twenty-four. He was at school on the Isle of Wight, and read English at Queen's College, Oxford. He was Gregory Fellow in Poetry, Leeds University, 1952–5, and has since been visiting Professor of English at Universities in Egypt and the U.S.A. At present he is a lecturer at a London college of education. His verse plays are collected in *Helen in Egypt* (1959), and recent volumes of his poetry are *The Blue-fly in his Head* (1962), *Selected Poems* (1965), and *Satires and Epigrams* (1968).

GEOFFREY HILL was born at Bromsgrove, Worcestershire, in 1932, and was educated locally and at Keble College, Oxford. At present, he is Lecturer in English Literature at the University of Leeds. His books of poems include *For the Unfallen* (1959), and *King Log* (1968).

KENNETH HOPKINS was born at Bournemouth in 1914, and on leaving school at the age of fourteen was apprenticed to an ironmonger. He became a journalist a few years later, and a full-time writer of books after the Second World War. At present he lives in Norwich. He has written novels, biographies, literary history, and criticism. Recent collections of his verse are *Forty-two Poems* (1961), *Collected Poems 1935–1965* (1965), and *Poems: English and American* (1968).

TED HUGHES was born at Mytholmroyd, in the West Riding of Yorkshire, in 1930. He was educated at Mexborough Grammar School, and at Pembroke College, Cambridge : the latter after two years' National Service with the R.A.F. For a time he taught in the U.S.A., but more recently he has been living in Devon and in London. He was awarded the Hawthornden Prize in 1961. His books of verse include *Wodwo* (1967) and *Crow* (1970). He has also written books of children's verse, including *Meet My Folks!* (1961) and *The Earth-Owl and Other Moon People* (1963), and the children's stories *How the Whale Became* (1963) and *The Iron Man* (1968).

ELIZABETH JENNINGS was born at Boston, Lincs., in 1926, and educated at Oxford High School and St Anne's College, Oxford. She has been a librarian, an advertising copywriter, and a publisher's reader, and since 1961 has been a free-lance writer. Recent collections of her verse are *Collected Poems 1967* (1967), *The Animals' Arrival* (1969), and *Lucidities* (1970). She has also published *The Secret Brother* (1966), a collection of poems for children.

JAMES KIRKUP was born at South Shields in 1923, and educated at South Shields High School and at King's College, University of Durham. He has taught English in many foreign universities, including those at Salamanca, Kuala Lumpur, and at three universities in Japan. He has written plays, autobiographies, and accounts of his travels all over the world, and particularly in the Far East. His books of verse include *Refusal to Conform* (1963), *Paper Windows* (1968), and *White Shadows, Black Shadows* (1970).

PHILIP LARKIN was born at Coventry in 1922, and educated at King Henry VIII School, Coventry, and St John's College, Oxford. At present he is Librarian at the University of Hull. He has published two novels, *Jill* (revised edition, 1964), and *A Girl in Winter* (1947); and his books of verse are *The North Ship* (1945), *The Less Deceived* (1955), and *The Whitsun Weddings* (1964). He received the Arts Council Triennial Award for Poetry in 1965, and was awarded the Queen's Gold Medal for Poetry in the same year.

PETER LEVI, S.J., was born in Ruislip, Middlesex, in 1931. His father was a carpet importer and so was his grandfather. He went to boarding-schools in Somerset and Berkshire. The members of his family were practising Roman Catholics, and at seventeen he left home to become a Jesuit. Later, he read the classics and Byzantine and Modern Greek for four years at Oxford. At present he is a tutor in classics at Campion Hall, Oxford. His books of verse include *Water, Rock and Sand* (1962), *Fresh Water, Sea Water* (1965), and *Pancakes for the Queen of Babylon* (1968).

C. DAY LEWIS was born in Ballintubber, Ireland, in 1904, and educated at Sherborne School and Wadham College, Oxford. He was a schoolmaster for some years, was Professor of Poetry at Oxford, 1951–6, and has been the recipient of many literary honours and distinctions. He is a Companion of Literature, Royal Society of Literature; he received the C.B.E. in 1960; and in 1968 was named Poet Laureate. At present, he lives in London, where he is a director of a firm of publishers. He also writes detective novels under the name of Nicholas Blake. In 1960 he published his autobiography, *The Buried Day*, and his *Collected Poems* appeared in 1954. More recent books of his verse are *The Gate and Other Poems* (1962), *The Room and Other Poems* (1965), and *The Whispering Roots* (1970).

CHRISTOPHER LOGUE was born in Portsmouth in 1926. He served in the Army, 1944–8, and at present lives in London. He has written plays, and made verse-translations such as *Patrocleia*

(1962) and *Pax* (1967), both from Homer's *Iliad*. The most recent collection of his own verse is *New Numbers* (1969).

LOUIS MACNEICE was born in Belfast in 1907, and educated at Marlborough, and Merton College, Oxford. He was a university lecturer, and later a feature-writer and producer with the B.B.C. He wrote many radio plays, and the last published collection of these is *Persons from Porlock* (1969). His translations include *The Agamemnon of Aeschylus* and (with E. L. Stahl) *Goethe's Faust*; and he collaborated with W. H. Auden in writing the travel-book *Letters from Iceland* (new edition, 1967). His *Collected Poems* appeared in 1966, and his unfinished autobiography *The Strings are False* in 1965. Louis MacNeice died in 1963.

EDWIN MUIR was born in Orkney in 1887, and died in 1959. He was educated at Kirkwall Burgh School. When he was four-teen, his family moved to Glasgow, where he worked as a clerk. Later, he became a journalist and a translator, as well as a poet. After the Second World War he was Director of the British In-stitute in Prague, then in Rome, and was Charles Eliot Norton Professor of Poetry at Harvard, U.S.A. His many books include *An Autobiography* (1954) and *Collected Poems 1921–1958* (1960).

NORMAN NICHOLSON was born at Millom, Cumberland, and still lives in the house where he was born in 1914. He was edu-cated at local schools. His books of verse include *The Pot Geranium* (1954) and *Selected Poems* (1966). He has also written a number of verse-plays, including *The Old Man of the Mountains* (1946), which tells the story of Elijah set in Cumberland. More recent plays are *A Match for the Devil* (1955) and *Birth by Drowning* (1960). Among his other books are literary studies, novels, and topographical works about the region where he lives.

RUTH PITTER was born in Ilford, Essex, in 1897, and was edu-cated at Downsall Elementary School, Ilford, and at Coburn School, Bow, E. Both her parents were schoolteachers, and she began to write verses at about the age of five. She was awarded the Hawthornden Prize in 1938, received the William Heinemann Award in 1954, and the Queen's Gold Medal for Poetry in 1955. Among her many books of verse are *Still by Choice* (1966) and *Poems 1926–1966* (1968).

JOHN PRESS was born at Norwich in 1920, educated at King Edward VI School, Norwich, and Corpus Christi College, Cambridge. He served in the Royal Artillery, 1940–5: mainly in East Africa. He joined the British Council in 1946, holding appointments in Athens, Salonika, Madras, Colombo, Birmingham, and Cambridge. At present, he is Deputy Representative, British Council, Paris, and also Assistant Cultural Attaché at the British Embassy there. His books of criticism include *Rule and Energy* (1963) and *A Map of Modern English Verse* (1969). He has published two books of verse: *Uncertainties* (1956) and *Guy Fawkes' Night* (1959).

SIR HERBERT READ, D.S.O., M.C., was born in 1893 in the North Riding of Yorkshire, the son of a farmer. He was educated at various schools in Yorkshire and at the University of Leeds. He served as an Infantry Officer with the Yorkshire Regiment (The Green Howards) in the First World War. Afterwards, he was an Assistant Keeper at the Victoria and Albert Museum, London, for ten years. Then he became in turn a professor of the history of art, the editor of an art journal, and finally a publisher. He wrote many books on art, volumes of reminiscences and of literary criticism, and one novel, in addition to several collections of poetry. His *Collected Poems* appeared in 1946, and *Moon's Farm* in 1955. Sir Herbert Read died in 1968.

JAMES REEVES was born in London in 1909, and educated at Stowe and at Jesus College, Cambridge. He was a schoolmaster, and lectured in colleges of education, 1933–52, since when he has been a free-lance author and editor. He has edited many anthologies of verse, and made two studies of English folk-song in *The Idiom of the People* (1958) and *The Everlasting Circle* (1960). His *Collected Poems* appeared in 1960, and more recent collections of his poetry are *The Questioning Tiger* (1964), *Selected Poems* (1967), and *Poems, Subsong* (1969). James Reeves has also written a large number of books of stories and poems for children. His home is at Lewes, in Sussex.

ALAN ROSS was born in Calcutta in 1922, and was educated at Haileybury, and St John's College, Oxford. He served in the Royal Navy, 1942–7. He is married with one son, and lives near Hassocks, Sussex. Alan Ross played cricket and squash for Oxford University and the Royal Navy, and has written books on sport and travel, as well as for young readers. He is also well-known as a writer on cricket for *The Observer*, and since 1961 has edited a literary journal, *The London Magazine*. A recent collection of his verse is *Poems 1942–67* (1967).

A. L. ROWSE was born at St Austell, Cornwall, in 1903, and was educated locally and at Christ Church, Oxford. He has published many books of historical studies, and is an authority on the Tudor period. He is a Fellow of All Souls College, Oxford, and Senior Research Associate at the Huntington Library, San Marino, California. Two volumes of his autobiography are *A Cornish Childhood* (1942) and *A Cornishman at Oxford* (1965). Among his books of verse are *Poems Partly American* (1959) and *Poems of Cornwall and America* (1967).

JON SILKIN was born in London in 1930, and was evacuated to Wales during the Second World War. Later, he was at Leeds University. At present he lives in Newcastle-upon-Tyne. He is founder and co-editor of the literary magazine *Stand*, and he has lectured at universities in the U.S.A. He was Gregory Fellow in Poetry at Leeds University 1959–60, and received the Geoffrey Faber Memorial Award in 1966. Recent collections of his verse are *Nature with Man* (1965) and *Poems New and Selected* (1966).

DAME EDITH SITWELL, D.B.E., born in 1887 at Scarborough, and educated privately, was Hon. Litt.D. (Leeds), 1948, Hon. D.Litt (Durham), 1948, (Oxford), 1951, (Sheffield), 1955. Her biographies include lives of Alexander Pope, Queen Victoria, and Queen Elizabeth I. She wrote many books of poetry and criticism, and edited *The Atlantic Book of English and American Poetry* (1959). Her *Collected Poems* appeared in 1957, and her *Selected Letters* in 1970. Dame Edith Sitwell died in 1964.

SIR OSBERT SITWELL was born in London in 1892, and died in 1969. He always maintained that he was educated during the holidays from Eton. He served in the Grenadier Guards, 1912–19. As well as poetry, he wrote novels, essays, short-stories, art-criticism, and five volumes of autobiography: *Left Hand, Right Hand!* (1945), *The Scarlet Tree* (1946), *Great Morning* (1948), *Laughter in the Next Room* (1949), and *Noble Essences* (1950). In 1959 he published *Fee Fi Fo Fum!* a book of fairy stories, his *Tales My Father Taught Me* appeared in 1962, and *Pound Wise* in 1963.

Collections of his verse include *Wrack at Tidesend* (1952) and *On the Continent* (1958). His last published book of verse was *Poems of People, or England Reclaimed* (1965). He wrote of himself in *Who's Who*, 'For the past thirty years has conducted, in conjunction with his brother and sister, a series of skirmishes and hand-to-hand battles against the Philistine. Though outnumbered, has occasionally succeeded in denting the line, though not without damage to himself.'

STEVIE SMITH was born at Hull in 1902, but came to London at the age of four to what is now a suburb but was then a country place with woods, farms, fields, and streams. She has lived there ever since, and was educated at Palmers Green High School, and the North London Collegiate School for Girls. Before becoming a full-time writer in 1953, she worked in a publisher's office. Her novels include *Novel on Yellow Paper* (1936), *Over the Frontier* (1938), and *The Holiday* (1950). Books of her poems and drawings include *Not Waving but Drowning* (1957), *Selected Poems* (1962), and *The Frog Prince and Other Poems* (1966). She was awarded the Queen's Gold Medal for Poetry in 1969. She died in 1971.

STEPHEN SPENDER was born in London in 1909, and educated at University College School there, and University College, Oxford. He served as a fireman in the National Fire Service, 1941–4. He was co-editor (with Cyril Connolly) of *Horizon* (1939–41), one of the most famous literary periodicals published during and after the Second World War. From 1953 to 1967 he was co-editor of the magazine *Encounter*. In 1951 he published his autobiography *World Within World* and his *Selected Poems* appeared in 1965. Since 1970 he has held the Chair of English Literature at University College, London.

L. A. G. STRONG was born at Plymouth in 1896, and was educated at the Hoe Preparatory School, Plymouth, Brighton College, and Wadham College, Oxford. He was a schoolmaster for several years before becoming a full-time writer. Also a novelist and a biographer, he published his collected poems, *The Body's Imperfection*, in 1957, and his autobiography, *Green Memory*, appeared posthumously in 1961. He died in 1958.

HAL SUMMERS was born in Bradford, Yorkshire, in 1911, and was educated at Fettes College, Edinburgh, and Trinity College,

121

Oxford. He taught for a while before becoming a Civil Servant in 1935. His books of verse include *Smoke After Flame* (1944), *Hinterland* (1947), and *Visions of Time* (1952).

DYLAN THOMAS was born in Swansea in 1914, and educated at Swansea Grammar School. His first collection, *Eighteen Poems*, appeared in 1934. He also published books of essays and of stories, including *Portrait of the Artist as a Young Dog* (1940). He was awarded the William Foyle Poetry Prize for his *Collected Poems 1934–1952* (1952). The first broadcast in full of his play for voices *Under Milk Wood* was given by the B.B.C. on 25th January 1954. When the play was read in the U.S.A. in 1953, Dylan Thomas himself played the parts of the First Voice and the Rev. Eli Jenkins. Dylan Thomas died in New York in 1953, and is buried at Laugharne, a village in Carmarthenshire, Wales, where he made his last home.

R. S. THOMAS was born in Cardiff in 1913. He is Vicar of St Michael's, Eglwysfach in Cardiganshire, Wales. He was awarded the Queen's Gold Medal for Poetry in 1964, and the Welsh Arts Council Award for Poetry 1967–8. Recent collections of his verse are *Pietà* (1966) and *Not That He Brought Flowers* (1968). He also edited *The Batsford Book of Country Verse* (1961) and *The Penguin Book of Religious Verse* (1963).

ANTHONY THWAITE was born in Chester in 1930, and educated at Kingswood School, Bath, and Christ Church, Oxford. He has taught at universities in Japan and Libya, was a B.B.C. radio producer for four years, and was Literary Editor of *The Listener*. Since 1968 he has been Literary Editor of the *New Statesman*. He is married with four daughters, and lives at Richmond, Surrey. His books of verse include *The Owl in the Tree* (1963) and *The Stones of Emptiness* (1967). He has also published books of literary criticism and travel, including *The Deserts of Hesperides* (travel in Libya, 1969). He was awarded the Richard Hillary Prize in 1968.

HENRY TREECE was born at Wednesbury, Staffordshire, in 1911, and educated at the High School, Wednesbury, and Birmingham University. He was Captain of University Boxing, worked as a teacher, then became a Flight Lieutenant on bombers in the wartime R.A.F. He wrote novels and literary criticism, and his many books for young readers include *Horned Helmet* (1963),

The Children's Crusade (1964), and *The Dream-Time* (1967). Collections of his verse include *The Black Seasons* (1945), *The Haunted Garden* (1947), and *The Exiles* (1952). Henry Treece died in 1966.

JOHN WAIN was born at Stoke-on-Trent, Staffordshire, in 1925, and was educated at The High School, Newcastle-under-Lyme, and St John's College, Oxford. He was a university lecturer until 1955, when he resigned in order to become a free-lance writer. He has written novels and literary criticism, and recent collections of his verse are *Wildtrack* (1965) and *Letters to Five Artists* (1969). At present, he lives in Oxford.

VERNON WATKINS was born at Maesteg, Glamorgan, in 1906, and was educated at Repton, and Magdalene College, Cambridge. He became a bank clerk in 1925, and was for nearly 40 years at the same branch of Lloyds Bank in St Helen's Road, Swansea. He served in the R.A.F. 1941–6. He was married, with five children, and lived on the Gower Coast, near Swansea. In 1966 he was the recipient of the first Calouste Gulbenkian Fellowship of Poetry at University College, Swansea. His books of verse include *Affinities* (1962), *Selected Poems 1930–1960* (1967), and *Fidelities* (1968). Vernon Watkins died in Seattle, U.S.A., in 1967 while acting as visiting Professor of English at the University of Washington. His ashes lie outside Pennard Church on the Gower Peninsula in Glamorganshire.

LAURENCE WHISTLER was born at Eltham in 1912 and educated at Stowe, and Balliol College, Oxford. He received the first award of the King's Gold Medal for Poetry in 1935. During the Second World War he served first as a private soldier then as an officer in The Rifle Brigade. His most recent books of verse are *Audible Silence* (1961) and *To Celebrate Her Living* (1967). He also writes on art and architecture, is a designer of mural monuments and tombstones, and is an engraver on glass. *The Initials in the Heart*, a volume of autobiography, was published in 1964.

DAVID WRIGHT was born in Johannesburg, South Africa, in 1920, and was educated at Northampton School for the Deaf, and Oriel College, Oxford. He has published prose translations of *Beowulf* (1957) and *The Canterbury Tales* (1964), and three travel books on Portugal. His books of poems include *Adam at Evening*

(1965) and *Nerve Ends* (1969). As an anthologist, he has edited *The Mid-Century: English Poetry 1940–1960* (1965), and (with John Heath-Stubbs) *The Faber Book of Twentieth Century Verse* (revised edition, 1965). In 1969 he published *Deafness: A Personal Account*.

ANDREW YOUNG, Canon of Chichester Cathedral, was born at Elgin, Morayshire, in 1885 and was educated at the Royal High School, Edinburgh (where he won the open 100 yards three years running), and Edinburgh University. He took an interest in wild flowers while playing truant. This interest became a life-long hobby, and he has written two books about them : *A Prospect of Flowers* (1945) and *A Retrospect of Flowers* (1950). He has also written plays, topographical books, and literary criticism. He was awarded the Queen's Gold Medal for Poetry in 1952, *The Collected Poems of Andrew Young* appeared in 1960, and a subsequent volume, *Burning as Light*, was published in 1967.

INDEX OF FIRST LINES

INDEX OF POETS